52 WAYS TO Have Fun, Fantastic Sex

Dr. Clifford and Joyce Penner

THOMAS NELSON
Since 1798

NASHVILLE   DALLAS   MEXICO CITY   RIO DE JANEIRO

Dedicated to John and Julene Stellato,
our son-in-law and daughter, in celebration of their
marriage on August 28, 1993. May you enjoy a long life of
continuing to grow in love together as you learn to

> forgive yourselves and each other,
> quickly resolve hurt and anger,
> tenderly regard and care for your relationship,
> laugh and play together, and
> delight in a life of fun, fantastic sex!

Copyright © 1994 by Dr. Clifford and Joyce Penner

Published in Nashville, Tennessee, by Thomas Nelson, Inc.

Except where indicated, Scripture quotations are from the NEW KING JAMES VERSION of the Bible. Copyright © 1979, 1980, 1982, Thomas Nelson, Inc., Publishers. Those indicated NASB are from the New American Standard Bible © 1960, 1962, 1963, 1968, 1971, 1972, 1973, 1975, 1977 by The Lockman Foundation.

Library of Congress Cataloging-in-Publication Data

Penner, Clifford.
52 ways to have fun, fantastic sex / Clifford and Joyce Penner.
p.   cm.
Includes bibliographical references.

ISBN-13: 978-0-8407-3484-6

1. Sex.   2. Sexual excitement.   3. Sex instruction.   I. Penner, Joyce.   II. Title.   III. Title: Fifty-two ways to have fun, fantastic sex.
HQ31—P4462   1994
306.7—dc20   93-30468
                                                  CIP

Printed in the United States of America.

30 WC 10

Contents

Preface

This is a fun sex book! If you struggle with major sexual problems, the suggestions presented here will not fix your sexual dilemmas. Instead, this book is designed to fan the flames of an "OK" sex life into a glowing sex life that blazes with fun, variety, and intimacy.

This is a lighthearted sex book! Some of the experiences we propose are wacky, but we have found that wackiness often helps loosen up and lighten the deadly serious business of sex. Sometimes we suggest that you move your lovemaking experiences outside. But be careful! It's important that you protect others from exposure to your sexual activity. Being "caught in the act" in a public place may be more than embarrassing to you and disturbing to others—it may be illegal!

This is a nondemand sex book. Demands take all the fun out of sex. So if any experience feels like a demand, communicate that to your spouse. Then change or cancel that suggested exercise. Never engage in sexual activity if you feel pressured.

This is a silly sex book. Some ideas may seem too silly for you. That's OK. Just as no chef expects everyone to like every item on the menu, we don't expect every reader to find all our suggestions appealing. Try those that you respond to positively. Experiment with others that are on the edge of your limits. Make adaptations if there are certain components you do not like. Stretch yourselves to be sillier than is common for the two of you.

For many couples, learning to have fun, fantastic sex will work best if the woman takes the lead. But if the husband is the braver or more creative one, then he should initiate and lead.

One warning: It will only cause distance and turmoil if either of you uses any of these fifty-two ways to show the other one how hopeless or inadequate he or she is. It's great to stretch and grow but never when it's against your own will and choice. Because we believe this so strongly, in some weeks' exercises we've given two options: one for cautious types and another for risk takers. Even when we do not give those choices, you can always make appropriate changes on your own.

One way you might get a sense of each other is to each read through the book independently and rate each exercise on the following scale.

1. I would LOVE this one!
2. I would enjoy this one.
3. I could do this one.
4. This would be hard for me.
5. I would never want to do this.

6. Don't even **think** of it!

This has been a fun project for us. We hope you have as much fun putting our suggestions into practice as we had putting the ideas together and experimenting with them. If you have any suggestions for fifty-two *more* ways, send them our way. And if anyone does all fifty-two in a row, let us know. We'll celebrate your success!

Clifford and Joyce Penner
2 North Lake Avenue, Suite 610
Pasadena, California 91101

A New Start

It's New Year's Eve. You're at a New Year's Eve party at your friend's home or at another gala event or a church celebration or a small dinner. Whether this is your favorite holiday activity or your most dreaded outing, you feel a combination of excitement and anticipation as the new year rolls in—as well as that familiar feeling of exhaustion after the rat race of the holiday season. At the same time, there is a tendency to reflect on both the joys and the disappointments of the past year.

As you remember your sexual experiences of the past year, you may experience feelings ranging from deep contentment to boredom or even incredible despair.

Whatever your situation, plan to whisper into your spouse's ear at 11:30 P.M. that you'd really like the two of you to go home and welcome in the New Year alone together.

If you have dependent children, prearrange for them to be out of your home for that night with friends or relatives. If your children are old enough to be out on their own, ask them not to come home until after 1 A.M., then security-bolt the doors so you will not be interrupted by a surprise return of some household member.

Have your spouse park the car while you

sneak in and quickly put a comforter by the fireplace or in the coziest spot in your home. Light the fireplace, play some favorite music, and light some candles. Then, depending on your sexual situation, invite your spouse to join you in a time that is pleasurable and nondemanding for both of you.

You might pop some popcorn, fix a plate of cheese and apples, and pour your favorite hot or cold drink.

Cautious Types: If there has been tension between the two of you sexually, this is the time to acknowledge your part of that difficulty and agree to try to change that behavior. For example, if you've been angry about a lack of sex, share with your spouse your plan to be less demanding for sex and to propose more caring, connecting times with each other. On the other hand, if you have been avoiding or resisting sex, express your intention to regularly initiate the kind of physical closeness that is not violating to you. The two of you may want to wait until next week to work out the details of these changes, but right now you want your mate to be aware of your desire to change so that the two of you can have a close, warm time in your cozy setting without any demands that would cause tension. Once you've had your snack and a time of romantic chitchat, affirm your love and spend some time hugging and caressing to the extent that is enjoyable for both. Welcome in the New Year with your newly affirmed closeness.

Risk Takers: If you are basically satisfied with your sexual relationship, that is, if there is no tension between the two of you regarding sex, proceed with more vigor! Have the room warm and toasty. After a time of sharing and snacking in your cozy setting, begin kissing, caressing, and undressing each other. Take your time by thoroughly enjoying each other's body. Keep each other hungry for more, but freely proceed to a full sexual experience to welcome in the New Year.

New Year's Resolutions

This is the year to spark your sex life! Last week's suggestion led you through a special time together. This week is the time to make plans for how the two of you would like to enhance your sexual love life. With the holidays over, you're probably back to your normal daily routine, but we suggest that you don't go back to your "normal" sexual routine.

Plan a private time to talk about your sexual resolutions for the new year. Allow about two hours. (If the thought of two hours of talk time sends you bolting out the door, reduce the time to one hour or half an hour—or just fifteen minutes if that's all you can manage.) Schedule this time when you will not be interrupted and you are not fatigued.

Each of you might find it helpful to prepare for this planning event by reflecting on the positive aspects of your sexual relationship and also the areas that could be energized.

In your time together, discuss how you feel about the various dimensions of your sex life and what *you* would like, *not* how you want your spouse to change. In other words, use "I" statements rather than "You" statements.

Together, talk through your total sexual experience. How frequently are you having sex? Are you both content with that frequency? If not, what would you like? How far apart are the two of you in your ideal wishes for frequency? What would be a fair compromise?

What about initiation? What percentage of your times together are initiated by each of you? Would you like your spouse to initiate more? How do you let each other know your desire? How might that be improved?

What time of day are you usually together sexually? Where does sex usually happen? Do you feel private? What preparation is made? Do you prepare your bodies, the room, the mood? Would you like to? Which one of you is most likely to remember or to enjoy taking responsibility for preparation? Or would you prefer to take turns?

How physically and emotionally satisfying is sex for each of you? How could your satisfaction be increased? How much time do you take for your experiences? How is kissing? What level of arousal occurs? How freely is that arousal expressed? Do you feel emotionally connected? Do you talk during sex? Would you like more or less talking and what kind of talk?

What about the afterglow? How do you feel after sex? How might you be more affirming of each other during this time after sex?

Once you've talked through each of these issues, together write out your conclusions; these will be your sexual resolutions for the year. Refer to them at least monthly.

WEEK 3

Holiday Surprise

With the kids home from school for an extra day this week for Martin Luther King Day, plan a special time for them in the morning so they'll be understanding of your arrangements for private time later. If one of you has to work all day, the other one can arrange to "farm out" the kids for the evening to Grandma's house, a movie, or a close friend. When the husband gets home from taking the kids to their evening event, the wife meets him at the door in her overcoat. He needn't know immediately that she is wearing nothing underneath her coat!

Wife, let him know that you are going somewhere very special, a place he always enjoys. It's free, has no calories, and it won't negatively impact the environment. Keep the tease going as long as you can or as long as it is fun and you are comfortable.

When you have him thoroughly interested, shed your coat and lead him to that place. It could be the guest bedroom, the attic, the basement, the floor in the living room, the prewarmed or precooled pickup camper, or the backseat of your car.

Then begin the slow process of enjoying what brings both of you the greatest pleasure.

Creative husbands can plan similar surprises if the wife is the one who has to work all day or who serves as the kids' chauffeur. (However, if the husband greets her at the door wearing just a raincoat, his bare legs may give away part of the surprise!

Sexual Appointments

The first month of the new year is coming to a close. How are the two of you doing with your plan to add spark to your sexual life? As February approaches, many good intentions may fall by the wayside. The demands of your career and family life or the failure to make your sex life a priority can easily take over. One or both of you may be disappointed that the need for a spark continues. On the other hand, you may be proceeding with deliberate focus and high energy.

Whatever the state of your efforts to spark your sex life, we would encourage you to get out your calendars and make your sexual appointments for the rest of the year.

"Ugh, sex by appointment? No way!" you are probably saying. We would like to entice you to give sexual appointments a try. Not all your sexual times need to be scheduled, but plan one block of time per week that is just for the two of you in a private location. Use that time to try out the sexual event we have recommended for that week.

You may decide to alternate taking responsibility to plan and prepare for your time together. That's great! Whoever is the designated instigator plans the setting. *Both* of you prepare yourselves, mentally and physically. Talk about your expectations ahead of time so you go into the experience with similar feelings of anticipation. Plan ways to free yourselves of any demands either of you might feel in your times together. You know yourselves. Think about what demands are likely to surface. Then work diligently to prevent them from clouding your special events.

Remember your dating years. To whatever degree the two of you were affectionate with each other, physical closeness evolved out of your having prescheduled times together away from the other commitments of your lives. You were there just to be together. That may have included time to talk, to share an activity, or just to kiss, hold, and caress. It is so easy to forget how well that worked and to think that in marriage, physical closeness will just happen. Well, maybe it will and maybe it won't. For most of us, the quality of our physical relationship is greatly enhanced when that occurs by design.

Having said this, we remind you to keep your plans flexible. It is important that your scheduled appointments not become rigid expectations. Think of these times as you would other enjoyable events that you schedule into your lives. How do you work out luncheon appointments with friends or Super Bowl parties or other sporting events or going to the movies or having dinner with another couple? Sometimes these connections happen spontaneously, but most of the time a specific date and time are set. And what do you do when a conflict arises? You weigh the ease of rescheduling against the importance of both events and work out the most appropriate situation.

The same balance of flexibility and commitment can characterize the times you plan to be together sexually. Your sexual appointments must be a high priority without being a rigid expectation.

Try it! You'll like it! Sex by appointment might be the secret to sparking your sexual relationship.

WEEK 5

Ozzie and Harriett

Are your genitals "user friendly"? Have you ever named them? What is your first remembrance of your genitals? When did you first notice there was a difference between you and the opposite sex? Were you curious about that difference? How did you show that curiosity? How did your parents and other adults respond to your curiosity? In your home, what names were used for genitals? How did your family refer to urination and defecation? How would you describe your genitals now? What have they meant in your marriage?

Individually, take some time to write your answers to these questions. Then talk with each other about your responses.

Discovery of genitals begins in toddlerhood. It is natural for children to touch their genitals just like they poke their fingers into every other body orifice. When they touch their genitals, they learn that it feels good. If that genital discovery was allowed for you and accepted as a natural sequence of development, the touch of your genitals will be associated with positive, soothing sensations. If your hand was taken away and given a slap, you will think of your genitals as untouchable, maybe even a part of your body to be feared. Similarly, if your genitals were named with pride, you will have claimed them as God's creative work. If they were not, you may view them as not only untouchable, but also unmentionable. If you came to marriage with a sense of disgust or ugliness in regard to your genitals, that is likely what was communicated to you when you were growing up.

Within a loving marriage relationship, a negative association to genitals can be changed to a positive one. That can start with this week's fun sexual encounter. The silliness of naming your own and each other's genitals can have a profound effect on your acceptance of your genitals and your ability to share them openly and freely with each other.

This week, after you have shared your responses to the questions, start thinking about names for your own and each other's genitals. Have a good time exploring various possibilities. Always stay with names that have a positive connotation. For example, one couple named hers Toyota and his Pontiac because of the association with the current TV advertisements for these cars. (Toyota's was "Oh what a feeling!" and Pontiac's was "We build excitement!") Ozzie and Harriet are other names that couples have chosen.

Once you have found names you both enjoy, you can begin talking to each other's genitals by name. "How is Harriett today? Ozzie has been missing her." This openness with each other's genitals can bring healing and lightheartedness to your sexual expression with each other.

WEEK 6

Love Notes

As Valentine's Day approaches, warm up for the event by sending your spouse a stream of increasingly explicit love notes. Talk about what you want to do for him or her or what you would like to have done to you. For example, let her know you are willing to be her love slave to serve her in whatever way will bring her joy. Let him know that he can expect his favorite activity soon, but don't spell it out. Keep him guessing! By now you know what your spouse likes, so if it is fun for you, do a little teasing with it as the day approaches.

Both of you can send your messages in a word, a phrase, a sentence, a paragraph or a picture. Write your love notes on the bathroom mirror, on sticky notes, or in letters he or she gets at the office. Let her find the message in her purse or briefcase, under her pillow, or in a book she's reading. Write something in his calendar, on a three-by-five card and pack it in his lunch bucket or slip it into the *TV Guide*. Much of the delight in all this is the surprise element, so let the messages be discovered wherever they are not expected.

You can send a whole series of messages that begin with:

You are . . .

I love you because . . .

I'd like to . . .
I wish we could . . .
You turn me on when you . . .

This is not the time to bring up a topic that has always caused tension in the past. Rather, pick something that you know will be enjoyable for both of you. It may be that the most the two of you can both enjoy is not all that explicit. If you are the risky one, be conservative in your notes. If you are the hesitant or cautious one, take as big a risk as you can. Go out on a limb in your suggestiveness, but don't promise more than you can deliver.

Maybe your last note in the series could be attached to a pair of silk boxer shorts for him or some sexy underwear for her. Again, only do this if it is a fun aspect of your love life.

Valentine Treats

"I love you," can be communicated with words and actions. Both are *expected* on Valentine's Day! So what can each of you do to express your love to each other in a way that will be an *unexpected* treat? What did you do to woo each other before you were married? What has your spouse told you he or she would like?

Often, men will feel most loved by a physical, sexual connection while women will feel their husband's love by an action or expression that shows he took time to plan ahead and prepare a special treat for her. Unfortunately, the natural tendency will be to read this and focus on what *you* would like your spouse to do for you. But you will enhance the romance of your relationship much more effectively if you focus on what *your spouse* would like you to do for *him or her.*

Once you've decided what you believe would be the most special treat for your spouse, get into the delight of planning it. Enjoy the process of giving something on your spouse's terms without any expectation of getting something in return. *Your* Valentine treat will be what *you* do for *your spouse.*

Here are some questions to ask yourself:

Would my spouse prefer that I spend money or not spend money?

Would time together or a tangible item be more meaningful to him or her?

Would providing relief by doing some task that is normally the spouse's responsibility to be most appreciated?

Be certain that your Valentine treat will not cause tension. Even if the thought is nice, the actual expression may be negative. For example, don't give sexy nightwear to your wife if her lack of sexual desire has been an issue for you, because the sexy nightwear is really a message to her about what you would like from her, and that comes across as a demand. Or consider how difficult it would be for the spouse who struggles with a weight problem to be all excited about a huge box of chocolates. The chocolates might be craved and yet cause conflict with the spouse's ultimate goal of weight loss. Likewise, your husband may not appreciate jogging shoes if you've been pressuring him to jog and he has been resisting. Or your wife may have difficulty being joyful in response to an expensive piece of jewelry if you were not able to pay last month's mortgage.

Here are some suggestions for positive Valentine treats:

1. Complete a task that has been on your "Honey-Do" list for quite some time. Then leave a love note expressing your love as the reason for your actions.

2. Make reservations at her favorite restaurant for the two of you. Write out an invitation: "You are invited to join me at _____ for an evening of _____. _____ attire will be appropriate. The babysitter is _____ and is scheduled from _____ to _____."

3. If he has purchased a sexy nightie for you in the past, groom your body, lay the nightie out on the bed, have a bubble bath run for the two of you (or have the shower ready), and have the children stay at a friend's house for the night.

4. Write a list of all the qualities you love in your spouse.

5. Give your spouse a foot bath and a massage (if that would be enjoyed).

6. Instead of giving a purchased card, write your own. Either create your own poem or expression of love, or hand copy a love poem from a card or book. You might consider using a computer to create a card that reflects the two of you.

7. Take the day off and spend it together doing exactly what your spouse wants. You might spend it working together, shopping, playing, or in bed.

WEEK 8

Music for Loving

This is a great week to talk about and experiment with music. As you celebrate Presidents' Weekend, make love to the rhythm of your favorite marching band or something like Ray Charles singing "America the Beautiful" or a choir's rendition of "The Battle Hymn of the Republic."

Beyond that, experiment with keeping time to a variety of types of music. If classical is your thing, each of you can be on the lookout for pieces that build at your pace from a slow and steady beat to a pounding crescendo. Or, if you prefer, choose some that stay mellow and romantic all the way through. You creative types can make a tape out of a series of pieces that you can use to control the pace of your sexual experiences. Work on it together, or one of you make it as a surprise.

Similarly, if you are into jazz, rock, country-western, gospel, or elevator music, experiment with what you like, finding compromises that work for both of you.

Variety is usually the key. Sometimes you may not want to use music at all. Some of you will want to use music as a sound barrier if your room is right next to the kids' or if the walls are paper-thin between you and the next apartment.

WEEK 9

Talk It Out

This is a communication experience. During this week take an honest look at your sexual life and share with each other what you "see." It may be that the two of you have never candidly discussed your sexual experience, so this may make you a bit nervous. Talk about that anxiety. You may be surprised to discover that you both feel a little scared. It's best to have this discussion while fully dressed and away from your usual lovemaking location.

　　To help you collect your thoughts and feelings, spend some time by yourself writing about your sexual experience. Write a sentence or paragraph to answer the following questions.

Sexual Interest	What is it inside you that signals to you that you are interested in physical closeness?
Initiation	How do you usually express that desire to your spouse? What time of day and in what setting does that usually occur? What response does your approach elicit?
Pleasuring	What is usually the first physical contact? Describe the sequence of your

	lovemaking steps from that point on. Who does what, when? And how does the other spouse respond?
Stimulation	Which of those activities is most arousing for you? What tends to stimulate you sexually?
Entry and Orgasm	When in the process do entry and each of your orgasms occur? Who decides this? What is that like for you?
Afterglow	What happens? Who decides? What is this time like for you?
Change	What would you like to change in each of these categories? Be specific!
Problems	What inhibitions hinder your freedom to enjoy the process of being together? What specific problem that *you* experience (not your spouse) would you like to work on?
Plans	How do you plan to work on that problem?
Goals	What do you hope your sexual life will be like in one year?

Remember: These are very sensitive issues! This is not a time to beat up on the other person but rather a time to share about yourself.

Together, go through what each of you has written, expanding and clarifying as necessary.

You may need to schedule a follow-up conversation to complete the discussion. And you most certainly should plan another review in a few months to check how you are doing on your plan. If your sexual experience is not satisfying because of a particular issue or problem, many resources are available, including two of our books:

The Gift of Sex: A Couple's Guide to Sexual Fulfillment (Word, 1981).

Restoring the Pleasure: Moving Past Sexual Barriers (Word, 1993).

Laugh a Little

Humor can spring from spontaneous comments or events any time in the sexual experience or from well-planned surprises. It could be in response to something you brought to bed with you that you bring out at a vital moment. Or it could be in response to a meticulously planned event.

For example, in our sexual retraining exercises we often have a couple go through a time of simulating or acting out a sexual experience without arousal. It's not designed for humor, but it usually brings out the "ham" in one or both of you. Here's what you do.

In broad daylight or with the lights on, locate yourselves in a place where you can make noise. Lying side by side with all your clothes on, take your body through the relaxation process by slow, long breathing (ten breaths). Let the tension drain from your body. Now start breathing in and out together, inhaling, holding, and exhaling with a sigh five times. Let the warm breath come all the way up from your genitals as it rattles past your vocal cords with an "ahhh . . ." Practice, even exaggerating this, until both of you are comfortable.

Now take off your clothes and lie down side by side again. Relax and then slowly begin to make the breathing, movements, and sounds of a sexu-

ally arousing experience. Do not touch one another.

Let the breathing start long and slow, gradually increasing the speed, depth, volume, and intensity as you let the simulation build. You may
want to fantasize about the two of you in some
delicious setting or activity.

As you increase the breathing, increase the
sounds and the movements of an intense sexual
experience between you. Take turns leading, or
each of you do your own thing together.

You might want to signal when one of you is
ready to act out the climax of this event, then do
that together. If you burst out laughing, call time
out until you get control and then continue. This
experience not only brings levity but also helps reduce inhibition.

There are thousands of funny things you
can do if you let your mind go loose and respond to
your crazy urges.

A word of caution: Under no circumstances
does it ever build the relationship if the humor is
biting, becomes a put-down, or succeeds at the
other spouse's expense. The humorous experiences must be enjoyed by *both spouses*.

Spring Shopping

Spring has just arrived. Romance is in the air. It's time for new nightwear. So . . . plan to go out together to shop for sexual night clothing for each of you. Or it doesn't even have to be night clothes specifically. You might choose sexy underwear that you would like to make love in. Silk boxers are great for men. Women might like anything from a soft flannel nightgown to a sexy T-shirt. Those are great if your husband also responds to you in that attire. Do not choose something that is negative for either of you. The men may prefer that the woman buys a racy teddy or a garter belt to wear with net stockings, but some women feel like prostitutes if they wear that type of garment. For some men or women, risqué) garments present performance pressures. A beautiful silk nightgown or a sexy cotton knit nightgown with lace may be a compromise. Half the fun is looking and exploring together what each of you finds attractive. Focus on the enjoyment of the search. Discovering your similarities and differences can be an eye-opener and lots of fun if you do not get distracted by whose taste is better than the other's.

You may do your spring shopping on your lunch hour and have to go back to work afterward. If so, plan a follow-up time to "try out" your new purchases. If you have the rest of the day for each other, have a light lunch, snack, or dinner, then go home to put your new garments to use. Talk on the way home about what you would like to do together. Focus your discussion on what each of you would like to do for the other or how you would like to enjoy the other. Avoid suggestions that require the other spouse to do something for you unless one of you would like that direction from the other.

Once you have created your spring adventure that incorporates your new clothing, take turns enjoying each of your ideas. Each of you lead the sexual activity you suggested. Initiate this springtime with an added spark!

WEEK 12

Anticipation

Anticipation can excite your sexual relationship when what you anticipate is free of demand. Either of you can initiate the sexual activity to be anticipated. You know your spouse well enough not to set up a "demand situation."

For example, your husband is at work. You just got the kids down for a nap and you've started to read a romantic novel. You get turned on by the love story you're reading, so you call him at work and say, "I'd like you to be home by _____ tonight to help feed and bathe the children and get them to bed by _____ P.M. Then I would like to _____." You fill in the blanks. You may want to act out with him the part of the novel that stirred your sexual desire. Or you can create your own fantasy with him.

Or you may be away on a business trip and your husband is home managing the household. Your world of successful work and accomplishments is making you feel great about yourself, so you are ready to come home and have sex. But you know your husband is worn out by the stress of coordinating his and your home responsibilities. So you call home and suggest that he get a babysitter for the evening who will get the children to bed early. Then ask if he will meet you at the airport, so you can connect on the way back home. You might offer to drive to allow him to rest a bit. Describe for him the sexual time you hope to enjoy with him when you get home. Keep in mind that most couples need some reentry adjustment after having been apart.

There are many more experiences a spouse could create to solicit anticipation of a sexual experience. For example, the husband might suggest a night at a hotel and plan all the entertainment for the night. In fact, you could write out a time plan to give your wife to allow her to adjust to the plan according to her needs and desires. The anticipated plan can be mutual. Or you might call from work and fill her in on your latest fantasy that you would like to act out with her.

Anticipation of a specific sexual plan can heighten the spark in a couple's sexual relationship. We hope that will happen for you.

Dream Night

Most of us think of sexual fantasies as romantic or seductive. Those definitely add spark to a couple's sex life. This week, why not act out a funky sexual fantasy together?

You might want to start by reviewing past funny sexual incidents the two of you have had. Some may not have been that funny at the time, but now you can laugh about them. We have several of these, ourselves. Once we fell out of bed. Once we rocked the headboard so hard it caused the vase sitting on the windowsill above our bed to fall off on us, actually hurting us. Neither incident was funny at the time, but now both of them seem rather funky and we laugh about them.

You may put some cushions beside the bed and plan to take a roll off the bed onto the floor in the middle of intercourse.

Sometimes a couple's intercourse experience is traumatically interrupted when the husband's penis slips out of the vagina. You might decide one of you is going to orchestrate such a slip and see how fast you can reconnect.

You might come to a sexual experience in a funky outfit. Be a movie star for the evening. Choose one that your spouse adores. Or you could be a seventies hippie wearing a vest and beads only. You might come to bed wearing your sunglasses and beach hat and bringing suntan oil to pleasure each other.

Create the funky fantasy of your choice.

The Spirit of Sex

After having a few weeks of a lighter sexual atmosphere, take some time this week to connect your spirituality with your sexuality.

Most of us did not grow up associating our sexuality as a part of us that is good and of God. But remember: This whole idea of being male and female and becoming one flesh was God's idea (sexual intercourse originated in the Garden of Eden during the perfect, sinless state of mankind).

Take some time to talk about how each of you views God's role in your bedroom. Do you believe He wants your sexual life to be full of spark? Does He care for you in your times of sexual frustration and pain? We believe God is not only the creator of our sexuality and of the sexual union between a husband and wife, He is also vitally involved in our ongoing sexual lives when we allow Him to be.

You may want to spend some time studying what the Scriptures teach about sex. Back in 1968, Tyndale House Publishers released a little paperback entitled *Living Lessons of Life and Love.* Now out of print, it was a paraphrased version of the Old Testament books of Ruth, Esther, Job, Ecclesiastes and the Song of Solomon, which we loved reading to each other. The Living Bible paraphrases Solo-

mon in a similar way. This week, read the Song of
Solomon out loud together as it is paraphrased in
the Living Bible, or in another contemporary trans-
lation. Each of you read the part for your sex. In
other words, when the woman speaks, the wife
reads that to her husband. For example, in chapter
7, the wife reads verses 10–13:

I am my beloved's
And I am the one He desires.
Come, my beloved,
Let us go out into the fields; . . .
Let us get up early to the vineyards . . .
There I will give you my love.

When King Solomon speaks in that chapter,
the husband reads:

How beautiful your tripping feet,
O queenly maiden.
Your rounded thighs are like jewels,
The work of the most skilled of craftsmen.

What a beautiful way to express your love
for each other—a true gift from God.

Show and Tell

It's time to pull out that old Kris Kristofferson song from the early seventies "You Show Me Yours (And I'll Show You Mine)." As sexual therapists, it is amazing to us how few couples have ever taken a serious, unaroused (or at least unaroused at the start) look at each other's genitals. If you are saying "no way!" we encourage you to hang in there with us through this explanation of what you are to do. Then if you just can't do it, at least talk with each other about why it is so difficult. If you are unable to talk about it, write about it so you get some perspective on your hesitancy. Then maybe you can share your writings.

Here's what you do.

Agree on a time when you will not be interrupted or distracted. Bathe or shower separately or together, whichever is most natural and comfortable. You will need diagrams of the male and female genitalia (such as those in our books *The Gift of Sex* or *Restoring the Pleasure,* or in anatomy books or some medical guides). In a secure, well-lit room with diagrams of the male and female genitalia and some lubricant available, begin by examining the man. First identify the specific parts by comparing them to the diagram. Next note the details of the penis and testes, particularly the coronal ridge and the frenulum, or "seam," on the backside of the penis.

This is a hands-on experience, so look and touch! The man should talk about and demonstrate exactly how he likes to be touched. Sometimes it is helpful to have the woman put her hand over the top of the man's hand as he demonstrates what he likes. Then shift and have his hand over yours as he guides your hand in stimulating his penis in the way that is most pleasurable for him. The man should also teach you if or how he likes his scrotum and testicles caressed (very carefully!).

If this is uncomfortable for either of you proceed slowly, talk about it, and don't push. No one should feel violated! It would be better to skip this experience than to violate either of you. If one of you has been a victim of sexual abuse, this exercise may be traumatic or impossible. No one should feel forced. Express your reactions and take responsibility to protect yourself.

When you have thoroughly explored the man, shift roles. The woman should assume a comfortable position with her legs spread apart. You will need the diagram and a hand mirror. It is vital that the woman be in control of the pace and detail of this genital discovery. Note the outer labia (also called lips) and the inner labia. Spread them gently, using a lubricant if needed. Identify the clitoris, noting how the labia come together to form the hood over the top. See if either of you can feel the shaft of the clitoris located under the hood.

This is a good time to pause and talk about

clitoral stimulation. Most men want to go for it vigorously while most women prefer a much lighter, intermittent touch on the shaft or around the hood. Talk about what you like, demonstrate, and then guide his hand. Be clear in showing exactly what you don't enjoy and what brings pleasure and arousal.

Communicate very specifically how you like the opening to the vagina to be touched, entered, and stimulated by the penis and by his fingers. Remember: You are the best and only authority regarding your body. The man should always let the woman be his guide in pleasuring and arousing her. It does not matter what the books say or what another woman has said or what the man thinks. Each woman is always her own authority. Accepting this fact can free both of you to relax.

By this time in the experience, you'll either be tired of playing doctor or so turned on you can't stand it. So either hold each other and fall asleep— or go for it!

For Pleasure Only

Most of the time sex works best when both husband and wife enjoy each other's body. For a change, however, one-sided sex can be a real treat.

This week the wife will be passive and the husband will be active. Next week, you will reverse roles and the wife will be active while the husband is passive. The focus of these experiences will be learning to give and receive pleasure for the sake of pleasure—without any goal. In other words, orgasm or intercourse is not an expected result of this pleasuring. If *both* of you happen to want to proceed to orgasm and/or intercourse, that's fine, but do *not* go into the experience expecting either. In fact, it would be best to plan not to because you will be able to stay with the sensations of pleasure more effectively.

For the first experience, the woman chooses and prepares the setting and schedules the time to be with her husband. Choose music, lighting, and a location that most facilitates your ability to soak in your husband's touch.

Once you have everything set up and the time you choose to be together has arrived, invite your husband to bathe or shower with you if that would be enjoyable or relaxing. You can set the boundaries for that cleansing process. Both of you brush your teeth, use dental floss, then gargle. You may want to shave your legs and your husband may want to shave his beard. Choose a lotion, oil, or powder that you would like him to use to pleasure your body. Lead him to your pleasuring bed or the love nest you have chosen. Now it is time for you to lie with your backside up and let him take over. Your only task is to soak in the sensations of his touch and positively redirect him if some touch does not feel good or is negative to you.

Husband, as the pleasurer, your focus is to relax and enjoy your wife's body for your pleasure, incorporating anything you know she particularly likes and avoiding what you know she does not like. Think of radiating love and warmth through your fingertips and of taking in the sensation of warmth and the pulsation of your wife's body. Allow her to redirect you if the way you are touching her is negative to her. Caress slowly. Take time to discover her body and the kind of touch that feels best to both of you.

When you have thoroughly enjoyed the back of her body, have her turn over, then enjoy the front of her body. You may want to start by giving her a facial caress and then moving down the front of her body, not focusing on stimulating her breasts and genitals but rather caressing all of her. If she invites more genital touching, use what she taught you last week.

When you finish pleasuring her, just rest together. Hold and affirm one another.

Changing Sides

This week it is the husband's turn to be passive and the wife's turn to be active. You are changing sides from last week's one-sided pleasuring experience.

Reread last week's directions and reverse roles so that, as the husband, you will follow the instructions your wife followed last week to soak in the pleasure and positively redirect her if her touch becomes negative in any way. Likewise, your wife will follow last week's instructions for the husband and pleasure your body with a focus on both radiating love and taking in the warmth of his body through her fingertips.

Afterward you may want to rest in each other's arms and fall asleep together. At some time, talk about which role you enjoyed most, being the pleasurer or the receiver. Decide how you might incorporate one-sided pleasuring times into your ongoing lovemaking. Just make certain you each get a turn at being both pleasurer and receiver.

WEEK 18

Patting, Affirming, and Lingering

During Week 5 you chose names for your genitals. Are you still talking to each other's genitals? How friendly are you with them?

This week the challenge is to begin a commitment to pat and affirm each other's genitals daily. This can become a part of your going-to-bed time, your waking-up time, or any other time that the two of you select.

So many couples only touch genitals when they wish to produce a response. In the long term, genital touching then becomes associated with performance pressure for the man or "Oh, he wants *that* again" for the woman.

Patting and affirming each other's genitals establishes a positive pattern connecting your genitals with an expression of love and affection, and it reduces the expectation of pursuing sexual arousal, release, and/or intercourse. When we learn to enjoy each other's body affectionately without ulterior motives, then playfulness, freedom, and sexual desire increase. Sometimes the one being patted may even ask the other to linger a little longer!

Prioritize

If you are going to keep the spark alive in your sexual relationship over a lifetime, you will find it beneficial not only to learn to enjoy a variety of sexual encounters but also to have times set aside to evaluate and talk about your sexual relationship. This week is one more of these times.

Plan a time this week for the two of you to have an hour or two uninterrupted and away from the bedroom. Before that time, each of you write down your priorities for your sexual relationship. What would you like to have happening in your sexual life? How could the two of you make that happen? What would be required of you? Where do you see sex fitting into your total relationship? Are there other relationship issues that are affecting your sexual life? How might you work on those? How often would you like to be together sexually? Does that include intercourse? Who would you like to initiate at these times? What demands have crept into your sexual times that are taking away your sexual joy? How might you remove these demands?

At your scheduled talk time, bring your responses to these questions. Take turns sharing an item on each of your lists. When you are the listener, try to really understand what your spouse is saying and feeling. Reflect back to him or her what you hear by repeating, in your own words, what you believe your spouse meant. Try to avoid thinking about what *you* want to say while your spouse is trying to let you in on his or her world. You will get your turn.

When you've talked through all of the items on each of your lists, compare your similarities and differences. Then compile a joint list that includes both of your suggestions. If the two of you mentioned something similar as an issue but said it differently, try to reword the issue so that both of your ideas are reflected in that one item. Negotiate how to include any of your differences. So often couples negotiate differences and work out compromises in other areas of life. Try to do the same with sex.

Once you have compiled a mutually acceptable joint list, prioritize it. Each of you number the items in order of your priority. Then compare your numbers. Affirm your similarities and discuss your differences. Try to create a prioritized list that is acceptable to both of you.

Make a plan for how you will put this list into action. Each of you take certain items that you will be responsible to initiate. Schedule follow-up review sessions to see how your prioritizing is making a difference. You might have a "checkup" once a month. Unless couples make their sexual relationship a priority, it often loses its spark because it gets only leftover energy.

Setting the Scene

Varying the setting for sex adds spark and dispels the humdrum routine that often sets in during the long-term sexual relationship of married couples. The variations do not need to be expensive or take much energy. Even a minor change can create a whole new perspective.

Take some time together to brainstorm about criteria for creating a tantalizing atmosphere for your sexual experiences. Think of ways to appeal to all five of the senses: smell, taste, sight, sound, and touch.

Smell: Be certain to eliminate negative odors. Clean the room so it does not smell dusty or musty. You may want to open windows and let in some fresh air or use a scented spray, a candle, perfume, or potpourri. Burning incense may be too much for some couples, but others really enjoy that.

Taste may not apply to the atmosphere as much as to your personal interaction. Prepare yourselves so you both taste good to each other. Taste may also lead you into a sexual connection. For example, going out to a special dinner may set the stage that leads you to desire sex with each other. Preparing a special snack and enjoying that as part of your sexual time is another way of appealing to your sense of taste.

The **visual** appeal of your sexual atmosphere is vital. There is so much room here for creativity. The lighting can be varied from having the room totally dark so you make love by feel rather than by sight to having spotlights on certain parts of the room or your bodies. In between these extremes would be one candle or lots of candles, the regular room lights, a light at the bedside, or a light away from the bedside.

You can make visual changes within the room or select an entirely new environment. For example, you might change your direction on the bed or you might use the guest bedroom.

Sound can affect the mood and the rhythm of sex. You may want to play music you enjoy or play tapes or CDs of ocean waves, whispering breezes, or other romantic background sounds.

Touch is the key sense to be tapped for sexual responsiveness. The skin-to-skin contact of your bodies is the most essential touch, and it can be enhanced by lotions, oils, and grooming, but the feel of the surface for lovemaking is also important. Some couples like crisp, freshly ironed sheets while others respond to soft flannel sheets. Still others prefer silky satin sheets. Talk about what you like. Also vary the sensation by trying other alternatives. The sensation of the surface can be changed totally by making love on a place other than the bed. You can choose the floor or a comforter on the floor or pillows or a leather chair or a sofa or the grass or sand. The possibilities are many.

You can create changes for all senses by choosing an entirely different location. As long as you are assured of privacy and you protect others from exposure to your sexual activity, you can choose almost any location that would be positive for both of you. These could include your backyard, a tree house, a pickup, a camper, a van, or a secluded beach.

After you have defined your criteria, talk through the possibilities we have suggested and come up with some of your own ideas. Then plan a system for who will take responsibility for varying the setting for your lovemaking. You might decide you want to change one dimension each month and that you will alternate being responsible for that change every month. Or you may want to change more or less frequently, and you may both decide that one of you enjoys being creative in appealing to the senses more than the other does, so varying the atmosphere will be the responsibility of the more creative spouse. Whatever your plan, devise it so it works for the two of you.

Nonverbal Signals

All of us send nonverbal signals all the time. This is particularly true in lovemaking. We move toward or pull away slightly. We start or stop making noise. We increase or decrease the intensity of our touch. We thrust vigorously or gently or stop moving. The list could go on. Many other nonverbal signals are much more subtle. These would include how loosely or tightly we open our lips or our legs, turning toward or away from our partner, or opening or closing our eyes. Note that we are talking about voluntary actions.

Talk about and practice sending signals in three areas: enhancement, distractions, and flashbacks.

Some nonverbal signals that enhance your sexual life will be natural and spontaneous. Other signals need to be developed. A few weeks ago we took you through the show-and-tell experience when we talked about clitoral stimulation—so we'll use that exercise to illustrate our point. This is one area where the need for a signal system is almost universal. Many women report that the clitoral stimulation they receive becomes too intense or painful at certain points, but when they express this it breaks the flow. Either the man is hurt and stops all stimulation, or he thinks *he* knows what she needs so he keeps right on going. It is much less disruptive if this dilemma can be discussed ahead of time with an agreed-upon signal. Perhaps three taps on the shoulder could mean "lighten up on the clitoris," or the woman could guide his hand to the area that would feel better or show him that she would like faster, more vigorous stimulation.

So many times nonverbal messages (especially if they are corrective) cause stress. If, however, they have been worked out in advance, they are less likely to be taken personally and will, in fact, enhance the experience.

The signals that you arrange can mean "too much," "too hard," "too long," "not enough," "harder," or "more." They could mean "I'm ready for entry right now." Or they could mean "Kiss my breasts, not my mouth." There are hundreds of messages and hundreds of signals—so have fun designing and implementing them.

Distractions from lovemaking tend to occur more for women than for men. If you are a woman who counts the specks on the ceiling or the drips in the shower during lovemaking, or if you make grocery or to-do lists while your husband is stimulating you—you need some signals. These nonverbal messages should let him know that you are distracted and need to get active or at least change the activity. It may be that a word signal would be useful. For example, you may want to come up with some words like "Aunt Myrtle" or "Vancouver" to mean, "I'm distracted." This becomes shorthand for the message without going into all the detail. No questions need be asked. Both of you know it's time for the distracted one to get active. It's hard to be distracted when you're busy.

Flashbacks may occur if you were violated in your past. This could have been molestation, incest, physical abuse, rape, or hurts in a prior or present relationship.

Flashbacks tend to occur when the violating activity is repeated in your current activity. If you were violated with the man on top or in the dark or by his hands on your genitals or by oral sex . . . under certain conditions and at certain times it will feel as if you are reliving the experience. The flashbacks could also occur in response to the sounds of sex, the noises that are made, or just about any part of the experience. If repetition of any event from your past stirs up negative feelings, send an agreed-upon signal immediately. The two of you should have a plan that has been worked out in advance.

Whether it is designed to enhance your experience or in response to distractions or flashbacks, plan, practice, and use your signals once you've decided together what they mean and what course of action to take in response to them.

Building Intimacy

Many of the activities we've already suggested for you to enjoy with each other require intimacy. In contrast, a five- to seven-minute sexual event in which two people get aroused, are orgasmic, and have sexual intercourse can happen between two complete strangers.

How would you assess the status of your sexual intimacy? On a scale of one to ten, each of you choose a number to reflect your sense of where you are with each other. Discuss the reasons you chose the number you did. In your discussion, talk about yourselves rather than each other. Avoid blame by using "I" statements instead of "You" statements.

If both of you feel like you have as much love and emotional closeness as you have sex, and that the love and sex are very integrated for you, then you may use our suggestions for fun rather than to bring about a change.

One of the dangers of sexual attraction being the start of a relationship and of acting on that attraction early in the relationship is that couples tend to equate love with sex. They get married without really learning to be emotionally intimate, i.e., to love one another deeply. To build on sexual attraction and develop sexual intimacy requires learning to share yourself and to take time to really get to know the inner world of your spouse.

You might begin by setting aside fifteen minutes every day or an hour or two every week to share yourselves with each other. Think of sharing thoughts, activities, and feelings.

If you want to work more diligently on developing sexual intimacy, our book *Restoring the Pleasure* has a section on communication that would be the place to start. Then you could go right to the sexual retraining section and follow that step by step. There is no way to complete those thirty-two exercises and not be sexually intimate. Besides, you'll have fun in the process!

If you'd prefer to just read and discuss, there are two books we recommend you read out loud together: *How to Put the Love Back into Making Love* by Dagmar O'Connor and *Getting the Love You Want* by Harville Hendrix. Both will give you information and direction for building intimacy in your relationship. This will enhance your relationship in and out of bed.

Sexual intimacy is an essential criterion for long-term sexual spark. The flame will die quickly without intimate love.

Charades

Earlier in the year, you read the Song of Solomon to each other. This week you can act it out! Each of you choose a verse or a section. Act it out and see if the other can guess which passage you are depicting. Have fun!

You might also find a love poem or a nursery rhyme to pantomime that could add some spark to your sex life.

There are other ways of playing sexual charades with each other. You might play a part or take on a role rather than act out a situation. For example, if you are usually the sexually aggressive one in your relationship, play the "hard-to-get" role. On the other hand, if you are not usually aggressive, be aggressive. If you are sexually extroverted, act shy.

The criteria for playing avant-garde roles is that no one is violated or put down, it is done for fun and tease only, and it enhances *your* relationship. *Never* should one of you feel a demand to play a role that belittles you or taps into past trauma or violates your moral stance (even though it's just the two of you involved).

Keep this experience light, playful, and full of intrigue.

Sexual Reading

Read a good love book together. We find it is most helpful for couples to read out loud to one another. The book you chose might focus on sex, intimacy, the marital relationship in general, or on a specific issue that would enhance your lovemaking. Read one chapter per night for as many nights in the week as you can manage. Not all the books listed here consistently agree with the values we promote, but they do provide valuable information.

Leo Buscaglia. *Loving Each Other*. Winston, N.Y.: Holt, Rinehart, and Winston, 1984.

William Cane. *The Art of Kissing*. New York: St. Martin's Press, 1991.

Joseph P. Dillow. *Solomon on Sex*. Nashville: Thomas Nelson, 1977.

James Dobson. *Love for a Lifetime*. Portland, Oreg.: Multnomah, 1987.

Harville Hendrix. *Getting the Love You Want: A Guide for Couples*. New York: Harper and Row, 1990.

Julia Heiman and Joseph LoPiccolo. *Becoming Orgasmic*. New York: Prentice Hall, 1988.

Alan Loy McGinnis. *The Romance Factor*. New York: Harper and Row, 1982.

Clifford and Joyce Penner. *Sex Facts for the Family*.

Dallas: Word, 1992. (A book for keeping the sexual spark alive thorugh all phases of life. Topics include aging, birth control, children's impact on couple's sex lives, infertility, pregnancy and sex, and talking to kids about sex.)

Clifford and Joyce Penner. *Restoring the Pleasure: Moving Past Sexual Barriers.* Dallas: Word, 1993.

Clifford and Joyce Penner. *The Gift of Sex: A Couple's Guide to Sexual Fulfillment.* Dallas: Word, 1981.

Gary Smalley and John Trent. *The Language of Love.* Colorado Springs: Focus on the Family, 1988.

Lewis B. Smedes. *Love Within Limits.* Grand Rapids: Eerdmans, 1978.

Ed Wheat, M.D. *Love Life for Every Married Couple.* Grand Rapids: Zondervan, 1980.

WEEK 25

Accouterments

Since it's the week of Flag Day, celebrate your heritage by pleasuring each other with red, white, and blue scarves!

Whether or not you use scarves, you can have a fun, creative experience by bringing three "accouterments" to your pleasuring time. Each of you choose items with three different textures, all of which would feel pleasing and sensuous on the skin. You might choose a makeup brush, hairbrush, piece of fur or fabric, silk scarf, feathers, rolling pin, facial tissue, toilet paper, or many other possibilities. Take turns being the pleasurer and the receiver. The receiver can get comfortable on his or her abdomen. The pleasurer chooses one object to gently stroke the other's back. The receiver should try to guess what the pleasurer is using. Do the same with the next two objects. Then the receiver can choose which objects he or she prefers. Pleasure your spouse's entire body with the different objects. Stop when you have thoroughly enjoyed yourselves, then reverse roles and do the same for the other spouse's body.

This is usually a fun, not necessarily arousing, experience designed to add variety and increase sensual awareness.

Semiannual Audit

It's communication time again. Time to stand back and take a look at what is happening between the two of you sexually. Has this focus on sparking your sex life been fun for the two of you? Beneficial? Or has it stirred up more conflict?

Each of you take some time to write down your responses to the above questions. Then look through the previous twenty-five weeks in the book. You might categorize each week's sexual experience as particularly enjoyable, beneficial, insignificant, or difficult. Then it may be helpful to group each week under one of these four categories. Do you note any particular similarity between the experiences in each category? For example, the communication experiences might have fallen primarily in one category and the physical sessions may have fallen into another and the creative activities in yet another.

Once you have each categorized your past six-month experiences, share your findings. This is an important process. It is vital that each of you feels free to communicate how you remember the experiences without being judged for your view and without judging the other for not having the same perspective. In order to most effectively hear and accept (not necessarily agree with) the other's viewpoint, practice active listening skills: Take turns sharing your thoughts and feelings. When the other spouse is talking, put aside your own thoughts, feelings, and ideas, and attempt to really understand *your spouse's* thoughts, feelings, and ideas. Deliberately focus on each other and reflect back to the other what you have heard him or her say. Allow the sharer to clarify, confirm, or expand on what he or she said.

After comparing your responses, identify the patterns you believe have been somewhat consistent for the two of you during the past six months. Do not focus on the time before this half-year. Only evaluate the prescribed sexual experiences of the past twenty-five weeks.

If the two of you agree that most experiences have been either fun, beneficial, or positive in some other way, continue on with the next six-month plan. Enjoy moving ahead.

On the other hand, if you believe this process has made no difference or has caused more turmoil, there is probably an issue that needs attention. This issue is apparently big enough to interfere with your ability to learn to have fun, fantastic sex. You may want to take your findings to a counselor. Hearing about the feelings these times together stirred up will be extremely beneficial to any professional helper; your reactions will help the counselor identify either individual or relationship issues that need attention. You may find that it is more helpful to put the rest of the book on hold until after you work through your deeper conflicts.

Then you may either start again at the beginning or continue on with the last six months' recommendations.

If the twenty-five experiences have brought joy and fun to your sex life or have kept an already fantastic sex life alive or uncovered the need for other help, they have been beneficial.

Fireworks

Are you ready for the Fourth of July? This is the occasion to bring your party hats, noisemakers, and whistles to bed. In Week 10, we guided you through an experience of simulating the breathing and sounds of sexual arousal and release. This week, you are *really* going to make noise.

The only hitch is what to do about protecting the other members of your household, apartment complex, or neighborhood. There are several possibilities. You might create a sound barrier by playing music loudly at the door or wall where sound is likely to carry to others. Or you can schedule your time together to begin at the same time the community fireworks start so that the combination of fireworks popping and dogs howling will cover your noises. Be innovative in finding an appropriate time, place, and setting to create your own fireworks.

Purchase red, white, and blue body paint to use in this event. Spread an old sheet over the bed so you won't soil your bedcovers. Be nude and freshly bathed or showered. Put on your party hats and any other patriotic paraphernalia. With your whistle and noisemaker in hand, sit on the sheet facing each other and begin body painting each other. Rattle the noisemaker when you like how or what your spouse is painting on your body. Blow the whistle when you want him or her to stop what or how he or she is painting. Have lots of fun, but also respond immediately to each other's signals. When the other spouse whistles, stop.

Risk

Many young couples today who have grown up witnessing passionate love scenes on television and in movies or have experienced sexual play connected with risk and guilt are disappointed in the lack of passion in their married sex life. They may even believe they have fallen out of love.

Only 6 percent of the sexual activities displayed by the media are between married couples. Sex is modeled as that intense, irresistible passion that sweeps you off your feet. Sex happens to you. Passion grabs you. But that is *not* what married sex is. When you can have someone anytime, you don't experience that adrenaline-based energy. Yes, there is passion between married couples. And, yes, sex in marriage has the potential to be freer, safer, less encumbered, deeper, and more satisfying than unmarried sex. But when there is no guilt and risk, there is no adrenaline-driven passion that many people raised with sex on TV and in movies assume is equivalent with love.

Understanding and accepting the difference between married sex and unmarried sex and between true, committed love and adrenaline-based passion is necessary to have fun, fantastic sex in your married relationship. Once that difference is understood, it can be fun to add a little risk, if that is done within the context of your marriage, protects your activities from others and you from them, and is energizing for both of you.

Sometimes the risk can be created by the setting you choose. We suggested some ideas for that in Week 20. You could also rent a motor home and have your sexual playtime there. Another possibility would be to go to a motel. Pretend you are sneaking away for a secret rendezvous. You might even choose a mirrored room or one with a private spa. Or you might plan an afternoon hike. Take a lunch, blanket, and lubricant, and find a safe, secluded location to enjoy each other. You may want to keep most of your clothes on.

Other types of risk taking can be created. In the middle of a well-attended event at your home, you may want to sneak away to your bedroom and lock the door. You may have fun putting a couple of thick towels on the floor in the bathroom and with the door locked have a "quickie" without anyone else in the household knowing. Keep exploring other possibilities. You may create new ideas between the two of you.

Positions

When people think about being experimental in their sex lives, the first thing that comes to mind is sexual positions. We find that sex is best and the sexual life stays most interesting when lovemaking is seen as an ever-evolving experience rather than one of getting "into position."

But to add a new twist it can be fun to try out some new positions. We recommend you do this without any foreplay or warm-up. Be sure the blinds are closed, the drapes are drawn, the door is locked, and the room is warm.

Cautious Types: Keep on all your clothes or at least your underwear if that makes you more comfortable. Then use a book that illustrates a variety of positions, or use your own creativity to experiment with the whole range of positions. Getting into these positions without proceeding to intercourse can be great fun.

Risk Takers: Take off all your clothes and turn on all the lights!

Both Types: Begin with the common position of the man on top. Keep in mind that even in this position there are many variations: the man's legs between the woman's, the woman's legs between the man's, the man straddling the woman's right leg or left leg, the woman's legs straight or bent at the knees with her feet flat on the bed or floor, or the woman's legs up in the air or her legs over his shoulders. Then try all of those positions with the woman on top. Even if all this activity is arousing, keep the experiment going rather than pursuing entry.

Next, try all of the combinations described above from a side-by-side position. Also remember when either of you is on top you can move from a totally parallel position to a sitting position.

Try sitting in a chair with the woman straddling the man (this works best if the chair back is quite narrow). Standing works for some couples if both spouses' height is about equal or if the man is very strong and can hold the woman.

If the man kneels or stands beside the bed while the woman's buttocks are right at the mattress edge and her legs are over his shoulders or her feet are resting on the bed, the man can move in from a low position, aiming at the G-spot (see Week 49), an ultrasensitive area on the front wall of the vagina. There are dozens of other positions, but by this time you'll probably be too aroused to try them, so go ahead and have as much fun as your bodies desire!

Morning Delight

It's Saturday morning. You are free to sleep in. You wake up with that warm, snugly feeling. To your delight you notice your husband is still sleeping and the kids are quiet. You quietly get up, go to the bathroom, return to the bedroom, lock your bedroom door, and snuggle up to your husband. You rub the parts of your body that are hungry for his touch. That could be skin hunger or breast or genital hunger that you go after. If he wakes up or stirs in his sleep and is receptive to your advances, place his hand on your genitals and your hand on his. As you are patting and affirming each other's genitals, rub your bodies together and kiss each other's skin wherever that feels good for both of you. You may want to avoid morning-breath kissing, at least until there is high arousal (unless you brought breath mints to bed for each of you). Pursue the arousal as long as both of you are enjoying it. That may lead to intercourse and/or orgasm. The orgasmic noises may need to be muffled so that you don't disturb others in the household. What a way to wake up!

This experience works best if the woman is the initiator. Most men would love to be awakened by a turned-on wife, but some women feel violated and used by being approached in their sleep. If you're a man and you know your wife would love this experience, just reverse the roles as we have described them. If you're the wife and you always sleep later than your husband, you can invite him to come back to bed with you. Or if he goes to bed before you and would respond positively to your initiating an "evening delight" when you come to bed and find him asleep, just change the experience to fit your situation. What you are trying to capture is that half-asleep, warm, cozy connection.

Kissing

Kissing is an indicator of the quality of a sexual relationship. When kissing is passionate, warm and deep, and when it's an ongoing part of a couple's relationship, they likely have a satisfying sexual relationship. It is rare to have a couple come to sexual therapy for help with their sexual relationship and have them report that they love to kiss. For the sexual therapist, asking about kissing is like the doctor taking your temperature to see if you have an infection.

Kissing is the most intimate and personal sharing of ourselves. It is reported that prostitutes and sexual surrogates will have intercourse with their clients, but they will not kiss them on the mouth.

Unfortunately, many dating couples bypass the kissing stage too quickly and move to breast and genital contact. Once couples can do the "real thing" and have intercourse, they usually engage in less and less kissing. Sex becomes more and more goal oriented. The passionate, long kisses become almost extinct. Then the sexual spark, pleasure, and intimacy die.

To keep your kissing vital and alive, spend this week's time together teaching each other how you like to kiss.

To begin positively, come to the experience having brushed your teeth, used dental floss, and gargled.

Select a time when you can have the living room or family room to yourselves and will not be interrupted. Put a "Do Not Disturb" sign on the door and unplug the telephone or turn off the ringer. Choose a comfortable sofa so you can sit side by side. Do this experience while fully clothed. Dim the lights or turn them off and light some candles. Begin by talking to each other about the way you like to kiss and be kissed. Use positive descriptions rather than talking about what you don't like. Talk about how your desire for kissing may be affected by your mood, your relationship, or the situation. Think about times when kissing was particularly great between the two of you. What contributed to those good times? How might you create positive conditions for kissing more frequently?

After talking about your kissing, take turns showing each other how you like to kiss. Alternate being passive while the other leads. The passive one is to follow the other's lead responsively, as a woman would follow a man in dancing.

First, use your lips to experiment with kissing your spouse's lips. Pucker your lips and gently peck across your spouse's lips and cheeks from one side to the other side and from top to bottom. Nibble by taking the upper or lower lip between your lips. Then reverse who leads and who follows.

Next, take turns leading in experimenting

with using your lips and tongue to find ways that you both enjoy interacting with each other's lips and tongues. This can include pecking, nibbling, licking, sucking, and thrusting, but keep the interaction soft and experimental.

Eventually, the involvement with each other's mouth can become mutual, simultaneous enjoyment if that is comfortable for both of you. If one of you becomes too intense or forceful for the other, gently remind the intense one that you'd like to keep it soft, safe, and experimental.

Plan to spend some time each week just kissing each other in a way you both enjoy. Never let your kissing fade away. Keep it alive and passionate.

House Swap

The kids are spending the night out or are off at summer camp. You're on your own and need a night "out" yourself. But you're also in the mood to try something different; you're looking for a change of scenery.

A fun way to get away with little expense is a house swap.

For this to work, you need to have some *good* friends leaving town for vacation, who feel comfortable leaving you with the keys to their house. Let them know what your plans are to make sure they are onboard with your idea.

Let your wife or husband know before leaving for work that you have a special evening planned. You may want to put a note in your spouse's briefcase inviting her or him to an evening out.

Sometime before the evening pack a bag with pajamas, lingerie, and a change of clothes for the two of you. You may want to include scented bath soaps, candles, some tapes or CD's (be sure your friend has a stereo system for these) with your favorite music, and two crystal goblets. Go by your friends' house (if they have already left) and stock it with tasty snacks and drinks and drop off your bags.

Meet your wife or husband after work with a mysterious smile and the promise of an evening of surprises.

You can go straight to your friends' house. Or you can take your time. Include a progressive dinner in your evening plans, hinting often of surprises to come so suspense will build.

Start off with hors d'oeuvres at a restaurant you haven't tried yet. As you finish your first course, mention you have special plans for dessert. Then go to another restaurant for your main course.

When you've finished dinner, tell your spouse you'd like to go for a drive before dessert. If you're behind the wheel, you can weave your way leisurely toward your destination for the evening. If you're in the passenger's seat, you may mention your friends wanted you to pick up the mail for them that night. Either way, you can make up an excuse about why you must stop by your friends' house: "They're expecting an important package and want me to pick it up and check on the house while I'm there."

Enter the house slowly, turn on the lights, and start to look around. "I wonder if they have anything to eat," you might say, heading for the kitchen. "We never did get dessert. Maybe we could have it here."

Your spouse should be uttering at least mild protests. But insist that he or she remain in the living room or den as you look for something to eat. What a surprise when you return with a lovely dessert or plate of cheese and fruit!

With the lights low, candles lighted, and music softly playing, you can enjoy your dessert together. You may want to talk quietly, commenting on what you appreciate about each other. This will keep the spark you've already ignited aglow.

You still haven't revealed the biggest surprise of all—you'll be spending the night at your friends' house. So you can suggest to your spouse that there is more fun to come. Then try this game, which Claudia and Dave Arp suggest for a romantic evening in their book *Ultimate Marriage Builder Get-Away Weekend.*

Tell your spouse you want to creatively share ideas of how you might make each other feel even better than you already do. You can write these ideas on paper, like coupons that you'll tear up and drop into jars or glasses. Or you can just say to your spouse, "Let's dream a little. If I could do anything right now to make you feel better, what would it be."

Take turns thinking of ideas or drawing them out of jars or glasses. After you have played a while—fulfilling suggestions like foot massages and back rubs—suggest you take a warm bath or shower together.

Lead your protesting spouse to your friends' bedroom and let her or him see the bags you've brought for the night. You may have even laid out your lingerie and pajamas. (Or, by now, you may not even need these!) Proceed to the shower or head straight for other things!

Variety

It's a hot sticky day. It's time for sex play, but the weather and summertime activities have left you drained. You need some variety to spark your interest. So what can you vary?

As you picture your usual sexual activity, write your answers to these questions on one side of a sheet of paper. What time of the day do the two of you typically connect sexually? Where does sex occur? What is the atmosphere? How do you let each other know you want sex? What is the first physical connection? List the sequence of events that is likely to occur in your lovemaking. Who leads? What parts of your bodies touch each other? What type of touching occurs? How are you each clothed or not clothed? What positions do you use most? How much and what type of verbal interaction is there between the two of you? How do you conclude?

Your sexual experience can be varied in all of these areas and probably in other ways that you might add to the list. To add variety to your sexual experience, take that experience apart. Identify all the various behaviors and conditions. Then list alternatives to your usual activities on the opposite side of the paper. In other words, opposite your answers to the previous questions, write what you might do differently. You might give just one alternative that you would like to try for a particular event, or you might write down a number of options to be tried throughout your life.

Here are some possibilities:

Time of Day: If you tend to have sex at bedtime, whether that is early or late, try a different time. Options include the middle of the night, early morning before the household starts buzzing, finding some private place for a "nooner," before dinner, or spending a full evening in sexual pleasure. Avoid the "after-the-late-news" rut. Be determined to vary the time for sex.

Location: Have you always been under-the-covers, in-bed, after-dark lovers? It is time for a change. If you can move out of the bedroom to another room of the house, that is great. Perhaps you could use another bedroom or any other room of the house. If the only possible location that provides privacy for sex play is your bedroom, then at least change your location in that room. You might use comforters, blankets, or pillows to make the floor comfortable. Maybe there is a chair in your room that would hold two playful bodies. If nothing else is possible, at least change your location in the bed. A new visual perspective often sparks a ho-hum sex life.

Atmosphere: In Week 20, we led you through the five senses as a way to vary the setting. What variations have you found most enhances your sexual life? Are the background sounds, smells, or visual effects most important?

Or is it the variation in taste and touch that sparks you? Choose one or all areas to create a new atmosphere. Change the lighting or the direction you face so that what you see is new to this experience. If you usually have a certain music playing in the background, you may wish to choose a new type of music or have silence. If you usually have silence, you may wish to play music or tapes of ocean waves or drums beating your rhythm or wind blowing. You may want to use a new cologne or perfume or scented oil. Changing the external input can greatly enhance the newness of your physical time together.

Connecting with Each Other: Catch each other off guard by approaching each other for sex in a new way. Interrupt his TV watching by appearing in high heels, a garter belt, and lace stockings (nothing else!). Give her your undivided attention for the whole day. The message you want to communicate to her is that you are hers for the day, and you want to please her every desire.

Getting Started: If you usually start with kissing, this time start with a back caress. Take turns. Or maybe you usually start by stroking one another's back; if so, then start with a foot massage. If you usually don't kiss until you are highly aroused, start by sitting on the couch fully clothed and kissing passionately for as long as you both enjoy it. Create your own new start.

Sequence of Events: Across from your list of how the two of you progress through your usual sexual encounter, rearrange the order, add a new activity, or change who does what. For example, if entry occurs before her orgasm, bring her to orgasm first. Or if he always ejaculates during intercourse, withdraw, play around, and bring him to orgasm outside your vagina.

Leading: Most of us get into a system of one spouse being more active in leading the sexual experience and the other being either passive or the responder. If this is your situation, switch roles. If he usually leads, the wife now takes charge and ravishes his body. Stop him every time he starts to assume the active role. Tell him this is your turn to be the aggressor.

Body Connection: Since it is the hot summertime, make love with the rule that only lips, nipples, and genitals can touch!

Type of Touch: Experiment with a whispery touch.

Clothing: If you are usually in the nude when you have sex, begin this time fully dressed and gradually undress each other. If you usually wear pajamas or a nightie, wear sexy underwear. If you usually wear your boxers, wear colored briefs. Wear something new or different to enhance your sexy feelings.

Positions: Review Week 29 or try new positions you think up yourselves.

Talking: If you are talkers, have an entire sexual experience without uttering a word. If you never talk during sex, take turns talking yourself through the entire event. Start with, "I am going to enjoy your _____ until you can't take it anymore." Then say, "That feels wonderful; now it's my turn." "Your hands on my _____ feel warm and firm." Model the lovers talking to each other in the Song of Solomon.

Wrapping It Up: Set a timer and stop when the timer rings. You might set the timer to extend or shorten your usual sex. No cheating. Keep with the designated time.

In the future, when sex becomes ho-hum, revive one or all of these guides to add variety to your lovemaking.

WEEK 34

Grooming

Human mating, attracting persons of the opposite sex, is associated with bodily preparation. What is viewed as attractive varies from one culture to another. In our culture preparing the human body to be attractive to the opposite sex includes grooming. Most of us were very diligent about preparing our bodies to be attractive when we were dating. We wanted to look nice, smell good, taste delicious, and be pleasant to touch. After marriage many couples become slack in maintaining their attractiveness; yet bodily preparation is vital to enhance their feelings about themselves, as well as their spouse's responsiveness to them.

Think about which grooming steps are important for you to feel good about yourself. Ask your spouse to define what grooming he or she deems vital. What enhances your attractiveness to him or her? For example, Cliff really prefers Joyce to wear dark lipstick, but the men of our older children's era often prefer their wives or girlfriends to wear no lipstick or a natural-colored lipstick. Thus, communicating what each of you prefers without being negative, critical, or demanding will be important to this week's process of learning to have fun, fantastic sex.

Bodily preparation serves several sexual

purposes: (1) It gets us in touch with our own bodies; (2) it helps us feel more attractive; (3) it makes us more desirable to each other; and (4) it can bring us together or be a connecting experience. To fulfill the last purpose, we recommend couples bathe or shower together as preparation for their sexual events. Personal bodily preparation that fulfills the first three purposes, is best considered in terms of the various body parts.

Mouth: To begin with, your mouth needs to be pleasant. Your teeth should be brushed and dental flossed several times daily. In addition, semiannual or yearly dental care is necessary to keep teeth clean and in good repair. Taking care of your teeth will help you have pleasant breath. Eating also affects your breath. Garlic, onions, fish, or other pungent foods can leave distasteful odors. Personal preference needs to be considered. You may not be bothered by garlic breath, but your spouse may find it aversive. Neither of you is right or wrong, but you need to take care of breath that is unpleasant to your spouse. In addition to regular care of your teeth, breath mints, gargle, parsley, and peanut butter have been used effectively to counteract bad breath.

Your lips are also an important part of your mouth from a sexual standpoint. To enjoyably share your lips with each other in kissing, make certain they are moisturized and free of sores or cracks. If you're sensitive to cold sores, you may need to seek medical help to treat and prevent them. Your mouth is a most intimate part of your sexual sharing.

Skin: Our skin is our largest sexual organ, so it must be clean and desirable to touch, taste, and smell. In most segments of our culture it is important to be freshly washed before we embark upon a sexual experience. That wasn't always true, and still is not for some people, so it is important to determine between the two of you your need for cleanliness. If being freshly washed is important for one of you, it is necessary for both of you. Napoleon, when he was coming home from war, wrote to his wife to tell her not to bathe for two weeks in anticipation of their sexual reunion. If you *both* enjoy bodily odor and it is a turn-on for you, that is your prerogative! If not, use soap and water!

There are other skin issues in addition to cleanliness. Dry skin should be kept moisturized so it feels soft and supple. Oily skin may need to be blotted. If you're a person who perspires during sex, keep a towel near you and wipe the perspiration as it comes. You might also try being more passive and relaxed during sex as a way of reducing the perspiration. Some specific skin problems can get in the way of your feeling attractive. If you struggle with acne, you may need to use a cosmetic cover-up after you wash for bed. Or if the acne is on your back, wear a T-shirt or a sexy top.

Hair: Hair can be an incredibly sensual accouterment to sex when it is clean, soft, shiny, and delightful to stroke. But body hair needs to be removed when that is a turn-off because of personal or cultural conditioning. Women in our culture usually remove their leg, underarm, and bikini-line hair (the pubic hair that extends into the groin and thigh). Shaving, depilatories, and electrolysis are common methods. Whichever one you choose, those areas need to be kept smooth and free of hair if that is important to you or your husband. Such grooming is as important now as when you were wooing him. If a man shaves his beard, he should be freshly shaven (unless his wife gets turned on by whiskers). For the man with a beard or a mustache, trimming, cleaning, and conditioning keep that facial hair sensuous. Nostril hair can be an issue for some couples. Sometimes women's pubic hair needs to be kept trimmed to prevent pulling for her or irritation for her husband. Take time to talk about your preferences and needs.

Hands, Feet, and Ears: In our practice, we often hear complaints from one spouse about the others' hands, feet, or ears. Ears are fun to nibble on if they are clean. If they are full of wax or dust or dirt they will be avoided. Hands that are smooth and clean with carefully manicured nails are beautiful messengers of love. Rough, dirty, jagged nails communicate lack of care, hurt, and roughness. Your feet may require professional care of a pedicurist or podiatrist if they are callused and unkempt. Or you can soak, oil, clip, and clean them yourself. Your feet can be extremely sensuous receptors, so keep them in shape.

Review individually, and discuss together, the importance of grooming for each of you. A well-groomed body is an instrument with which to share fun, fantastic sex!

The Ten Nondemandments

Anne and Gene had been through the whole process of sexual retraining in sexual therapy. Near the end they decided to renew their vows. They called them their "Ten Nondemandments." We liked them so much we asked to adapt them and share them here.

The Ten
Nondemandments

1. I, Anne, will be a safe harbor for Gene.
2. I, Gene, will be a safe harbor for Anne.
3. Anne vows she will "know" only Gene.
4. We vow to "paintbrush" regularly (see Week 39).
5. Gene will honor Anne's request to be held.
6. Gene and Anne vow to keep an unlimited supply of lubricant available.
7. Gene vows not to penetrate Anne until she feels fulfilled, or satisfied.
8. Anne vows to provide alternative experiences at Gene's request.
9. Anne and Gene vow to make creativity a priority, continuing to try various positions.

10. Gene promises to listen when Anne says things are getting to be "too much."

Your conversations and commitments can be just as unique. Let yourselves be creative as you write your own list of commitments.

Redecorate the Bedroom

No! You don't need to call the interior decorator. Nor do you need a no-limit bank account. We're talking about working with what you've got. It's Labor Day, so work together!

We have often said if you want to take only *one* step to make a radical change in your sex life get rid of the television set! This is doubly true in the bedroom. TV watching is an individual, spectator activity that a couple does side by side but not together. Watching TV rarely brings people closer to each other.

Next, get rid of the clutter! If your bedroom has piles of clothes that didn't make it back into the closet or the laundry hamper, clean up! Get rid of the stacks of old magazines, too, along with those half-read books, last year's tax receipts, or anything else that keeps you from knowing the color of your carpet.

And remember: This is a *joint* activity, not a job for one spouse alone. Then, clean! Wash the curtains or drapes and polish the windows. Dust the furniture. Turn the mattress. Air out the bedding and the room!

All this has been basic. Now you're ready to get creative. You can do that on the no-budget plan, the low-budget plan, or the no-limits plan.

The No-Budget Plan: Start by rearranging the furniture. Put the bed where the chest of drawers was, even if it's not ideal. You can always move things back in a week. Or turn the bed in the opposite direction, even if that means the headboard is in the middle of the room. If there is nowhere to move the bed, put it in the middle of the room or in front of the full-length mirror and leave it there for two weeks. You might ask what's the point? The answer is: changes! Why do we tend to get more sexual when we stay in a hotel or motel? It's new!

Move the lamps and the pictures. Change to brighter or dimmer light bulbs than you usually use.

Make the bed with the pillows at the foot-end of the bed rather than at the headboard. Find all the old, half-used candles around the house and store them by your bedside to be used regularly. Pick some flowers from your garden and let them add beauty and romance (but only if they don't make you sneeze).

The Low-Budget Plan: In addition to or instead of all the above suggestions, make some changes that require a little cash. Buy new sheets that have some zing to them, either in how they feel (satin, silk, all cotton) or in how they look (pastel flowers, wild colors, or zany designs). Get a new piece of fabric to cover the corner table.

Agree on how you want to repaint or paper

the room. Make your choice with your lovemaking as the primary guide. If one of you is much more sensitive to atmosphere than the other, go with the most sensitive one's needs or desires. Traditionally this has been the woman, but we often hear from men that this is a big issue for them as well.

Buy some wall hangings or colored lights if they do something for you. Buy some trays to serve each other breakfast (òr dinner) in bed. In all this, keep in mind you are doing this for each other, not for the approval of your mother-in-law or your best friend.

The No-Limits Budget: Completely redesign your bedroom to include a private spa, bathtub, and a two-headed shower. Go shopping for a bed that matches your fantasy of something romantic. Do the same in terms of drapes, carpets, and bed covers. Choose what is most pleasing to your tastes whether or not it happens to coincide with the current edition of *House Beautiful.*

Whether you're classic or creative, and whatever your budget, remember to make this a joint project. If one of you just can't get "with it," then the other one can take the lead, including the hesitant one as much as possible in the decisions.

Remember, too, that this is not a one-time event! Change little things regularly and make a major change once a year!

Moving Slowly

The words of a popular song praise the lovemaking techniques of men with a "slow hand" and "an easy touch." There's probably not a woman alive who doesn't agree. In our seminars, the women are always asking us to tell the men to "slow down!"

Somehow this concept seems to go against a man's very nature and certainly against his training. Boys are taught to "score"—the sooner the better. Get to the goal first and you win the prize.

But in lovemaking, just the opposite is true. The slower the better, not only for the woman but for both of you, because you end up together at greater heights of ecstasy.

Body pleasuring has many different functions: It helps us connect by bringing our worlds together, it helps us relax as we let go of the stress and tension of our day, it helps us get with our bodily sensitivities, and it helps us get turned on. Usually it happens in that order, particularly for women. If lovemaking is rushed, some important ingredients of a fulfilling sexual experience are bypassed.

First, consider the principles of pleasuring: All pleasuring is for mutual benefit. It does not come about as a result of demand, manipulation, or coercion. Pleasure is the goal, although arousal may be the outcome or consequence. Pleasuring is skin oriented, not muscle (massage) oriented. That's why we as sex therapists call pleasuring "sensate focus." The pleasurer gets as much as the receiver because the pleasurer enjoys touching his or her spouse's body in the way that brings the pleasurer the greatest pleasure. The receiver's responsibility is to communicate to the pleasurer about anything that is not enjoyable. Couples can add intensity to their pleasuring by always looking for new activities that bring pleasure to both.

As the receiver, your only task is to soak in the pleasure and redirect the pleasurer when the touch is not pleasing. As the pleasurer, you lovingly touch your spouse in such a way that feels good to you. Concentrate on radiating warmth through your hands. Take in the sensation and pulsations of your partner's body. Move S-L-O-W-L-Y.

Enough lecturing on principles; let's get to pleasuring!

Begin by bathing or showering together. This is a great way not only to get clean but also to connect. Men: avoid the groping and grabbing that is so tempting. It is a junior high approach that is a turn-off to all women!

Take turns pleasuring each other in a secure location where the temperature is comfortable without clothes or blankets. Decide who will be the first pleasurer or receiver. With the receiver lying on his or her stomach, the pleasurer slowly caresses the other's whole backside, including every square centimeter. Both of you soak in the pleasure as this head-to-toe caress continues. Then the receiver rolls over. Pleasurers, especially male pleasurers, are urged not to rush to the "hot spots." Think of teasing or making her beg for more breast or genital pleasure. Slowly caress the whole front side without a focus on the most erotic areas. If the woman usually has one orgasm per experience, don't push for it. As you near the end of the first pleasuring, include some stimulation, but even then tease with it!

Reverse roles and let the first pleasurer now be the receiver, repeating what was done on the first round! When both of you have been totally pleasured you can stop the experience, talk or fall asleep together, or move on to intercourse.

If you do choose to move on to intercourse you will notice that the intensity of the experience is much greater than when you have not taken the time to focus on the giving and receiving of pleasure. The arousal will be higher and the orgasm(s) will be more intense. As a result you may decide to include slow-moving hands and easy touching of each other's body in all of your sexual experiences. More details and suggestions about pleasuring are included in our book *Restoring the Pleasure*.

A "slow mouth" can produce as much pleasure as "slow hands." The principles and process of a slow mouth are the same as those for slow hands, only you use your mouth to kiss, lick, nibble, and smack on each other's body. When you are freshly washed and before you apply any oils or creams (unless they are edible oils and lotions, which can add lots of fun!), begin snuggling your face and mouth against your spouse's back. The back of the neck, the waist, and the inner part of the legs can be very sensitive, so guide each other to keep good feelings going rather than overload the other. Once you have enjoyed the back, enjoy the front of your spouse's body with your mouth. Then reverse roles and passively enjoy your spouse's caresses over your body with his or her mouth. Ultimately your enjoyment is a matter of taste!

All-Day Foreplay

How many times have we heard it? Sex begins in the kitchen! That doesn't mean you start kissing in the kitchen or begin to undress each other. It means this: If you want to have sex later on in the bedroom, you better start paying attention to her in the kitchen. Women regularly tell us, "He comes home, eats his dinner, and plops himself in front of the TV until 11 P.M. while I feed and bathe the kids, put them to bed, fold the wash, and make tomorrow's lunches. Then suddenly he notices that I'm alive and he wants sex." It leaves the woman hurt, furious, and turned off.

All-day foreplay for men is very different from all-day foreplay for women. Each gender needs its own uniquely designed and executed plan.

For the Man: Remember the answer to King Arthur's question in *Camelot,* when he asks how to handle a woman? The answer is "to love her and love her, just love her!" Most women (in contrast to men) do not respond favorably to "Hey, you want to have sex?" They do respond when they feel loved, cherished, helped, understood, encouraged, complimented, or adored. But this is not a one-for-one trade: "I'll adore you if we can then have sex." This is love without demands or strings.

The day might go something like this: It's Saturday morning. Instead of sitting and reading the paper, you help her by controlling the kids while she cooks breakfast. Then you help clean up and volunteer to run to the grocery store (which she was going to do) while she gets ready to go watch the kids' sports event. After lunch you watch the kids while she takes a nap, even if that means you miss a part of the football game. After dinner turn off the TV and talk (if she doesn't faint). Find out how she is doing, what she's feeling about your relationship, how she's feeling about the kids, or a hundred other topics. Then let her know how you feel about her. Offer to pleasure her in the way you learned in Week 37. Of course, you would like to end this day with a sexual experience, but don't expect it! Remember: If you are keeping score, you are way behind! You may need a week or a month of foreplay before she is eager. The focus is on loving and serving; the sexual response will be a delightful by-product. If a woman never becomes interested even after weeks of nondemand, unconditional loving, she may have a sexual barrier that needs professional help.

Men, remember there are a thousand variations to the day described here. You need to adapt this plan to your particular situation and stage of life. Your plan for all-day foreplay needs to be adapted to the particular woman you are married to.

For the Woman: Men are less complicated sexually. They don't do all that well with the indirect approach. Men need a clearly sexual *tease* or *touch.* Here's one way that could happen:

Start with a kiss in the morning that promises more as the day goes on. Control the length and intensity of the kiss or the touch. Perhaps you could invite another couple for a quiet dinner that night. As you are preparing your body that evening for the dinner party, lean out the bathroom door with nothing on. Keep his mind centered on you. Just before your guests arrive let him know that even though you are perfectly modest on the outside you aren't wearing any underwear! Then, as you serve your guests, brush by him in a way that only he will notice. You may be amazed how early he will bring the social event to a close!

Or . . . the two of you are setting off on a seven-hour trip. As you drive out the driveway you share a fantasy of what you'd like to have happen on the way or when you arrive at your destination. Set the timer on your watch and enjoy a new twist to your fantasy each hour as your watch beeps. Your approach becomes even more overt when you stop for the picnic you've prepared for lunch. When you finally arrive at your destination you both may not be able to wait until after dinner to enjoy your sexual time together.

Remember: You can be warming up each other all day. That is all-day foreplay in both directions!

New Ways to Touch

"No hands" pleasuring can bring contrast to the "slow hands" pleasuring of two weeks ago. Most of us depend on our hands to communicate sexual pleasure. Eliminating the use of your hands for this week's sexual playtime may stretch you a bit— mentally *and* physically! The purpose is to explore and discover other parts of your bodies besides your hands that receive and give pleasure when used to touch. Some attempts at using body parts may feel awkward. That is expected and not a negative. Have fun!

Spend some time preparing the atmosphere and your bodies for this fun time of exploration together. As the woman, start the pleasuring by using any part of your body to enjoy your husband's body for your pleasure. Make a deal with him that he will positively redirect you if anything you do is negative for him. As long as your touch is neutral or positive for him, you are free to experiment. He is to be passive and just soak in the pleasure of your enjoyment. Make this an experimental and fun time of discovering what parts of your body you enjoy using to touch your husband's body. You might use your hair, nose, eyes, tongue, ears, forearms, breasts, genitals, feet, or whatever. Start with him lying on his abdomen so you can pleasure the backside of his body. Have him turn over when you are ready for the front of his body.

When you have thoroughly enjoyed your husband's total body, reverse roles and you be the passive one while your husband enjoys using various parts of his body to pleasure first your backside and then your front side. As the husband, take time to experiment with various parts of your body for touching to discover which you enjoy most. Stop when you have thoroughly enjoyed your wife's body.

Since you may use your mouths, you may incorporate anything you found you enjoyed in the slow-kissing time, but don't limit yourselves to a repeat of that event. Also, the question of using your mouths to enjoy each other's genitals (oral sex) is usually raised with this experience. Discuss your feelings about oral sex before you start. If that form of stimulation is aversive to either of you or one of you would be violated by that, do not include oral stimulation. These times should never be negative for either of you. Fun, fantastic sex does not happen unless the activity engaged in can be enjoyed by both. If oral stimulation is enjoyable for both of you, include that if you wish. If you have never tried oral stimulation but would like to, as long as your mouth is free of sores and your genitals are freshly washed, experiment with little nibbles and licks as you find that enjoyable. Oral genital stimulation is not, however, the focus of this time together. The focus is to use all of your body, except your hands, to enjoy your spouse's bodies.

Each of you may use your hands for one purpose: to hold the penis, whether flaccid or erect, to pleasure the woman's genitals. Using the names you gave your genitals during Week 3, have them talk to each other. Use the penis like a paint-brush over the clitoris and labia and the opening to the vagina, a technique we call "paintbrushing."

Have a great time laughing and discovering together.

Sports Wives Anonymous

It is time for the major league playoffs and the World Series. Or it may be hunting season. Suddenly watching baseball games on TV, getting a deer, or shooting four ducks in a day becomes all-consuming. Often these are activities the husband enjoys while the wife feels ignored or left behind. If this is your situation, it can be a challenging time for your relationship. It is difficult to comprehend how a sports event can stir up that much emotion in your man—probably more emotion than he has ever shown in relation to you, at least since you've been married. As a result you may be feeling anywhere from slightly insecure to severely threatened. Questions race through your whole being and throb over and over in your mind: "Does he really *love* me?" "Has he lost his *passion* for me?" "Am I still a *priority?*" "Do I even *exist* in his mind?"

You are not alone! You may want to start a self-help support group for wives called Sports Widows Anonymous. This is a good time to review the differences between men and women. Some good examples are described in George Gilder's book *Men and Marriage.* To put it simply, men are conquerors; women are nurturers. But even "conquerors" need the relationship nurturing that women are more naturally equipped to give. Men are most successful when their inherent aggressiveness is channeled into connecting with their wives and providing for their families. So even while you accept, maybe even enjoy, his intense, captivating response to the "hunt," the competition, or the challenge to conquer and win, do not whimper away and feel sorry for yourself. Rather, take on the challenge of your role in the relationship. Make sure he knows you still exist and have fun doing it! But do not irritate him.

Let's say he's been glued to the TV for several hours. You really are hungry for his attention. Don't whine or complain. That will only make him feel bad about his natural tendencies and then make him angry with you for making him feel bad. Try an alternative solution: Listen for a commercial break. Each time there is a break in the game, bring him a cold drink or snack. Each time wear one less item of clothing or open your blouse a button or two more and be braless under the blouse. Then add his favorite perfume, lipstick, or hairdo. Don't be subtle about what you are doing. Make sure he notices, but keep a challenging distance, so that he has to "come after" you a bit. In other words, tease him. Play hard to get. Let him know where he can find you and what he can expect from you at the finish of the game.

For the "hunter's widow," your challenge of

keeping yourself in your husband's mind is slightly different. How can you titillate him with constant positive reminders of your existence while he is away from home? Have him begin his day by finding a note from you on his mirror when he shaves in the early morning before he leaves. Then tuck notes away in his hunting gear and food pack so that he finds them throughout the day. If he is going to be away for several days, leave notes in his underwear. Maybe even include a pair of yours. The same approach can work for a businesswoman away on a business trip.

Have fun with the notes! "As you shave off your whiskers, hear one whisper 'I love you.'" "Even as there is a deer to be hunted in the woods, there is a dear who will be a real challenge to conquer tonight when you come home." "When you're freezing your buns in the forest, remember your bun-warmer at home." Then you might describe what he might find upon his return. Create your own fantasy. We assure you, the positive tease approach to keep a husband connected is far more effective than the nagging complaining wife. But it will take your energy to nurture that connection and creativity to communicate it.

WEEK 41

A Delectable Feast

Whether you are in the United States celebrating Columbus Day or having Canadian Thanksgiving, why not turn the leftovers from your feast into a sexual orgy? Or if you have decided to spend this holiday alone as a couple, have dinner in the bedroom.

Start early in the week to dream and jot down ideas for your plan. Approach this event very much like you might if you were planning to entertain a guest.

First, prepare a setting that will allow for private, uninterrupted playfulness and creativity. Protect all surfaces from stains or damage. You may want to put down a large piece of plastic, an old vinyl tablecloth, a garment bag, or whatever you can find. Then cover the plastic with a washable blanket or sheet. Tuck it in or put weights along the edges so it doesn't slip.

If one of you is the chef in the family, this can be your treat. If both of you cook, make it a joint project. You may want to prepare dinner in *just* your aprons.

A great book to use this week is the *Aphro-*

disiac Cookbook (Surfside Publishing), by Bonnie Gartshore, Kim Collins, and Ann Peters. These authors suggest that dishes with a lot of mustard, hot spices, paprika, shrimp, or other fish high in phosphorous usually excite both men and women. Eliminate garlic, onions, or other flavors if they cause breath problems for either of you. Then cook and play!

Hors D'oeuvres: The meal and sex begin best with light nibbles. Cheese sticks and fruit-flavored sparkling water can be fed to each other. Nibble the cheese stick from each end until your lips meet and you enjoy another form of nibbling delight. Raw vegetables and dip utilize hands and mouths, both important "instruments" in lovemaking. Dipping veggies and feeding them to each other then licking off of each other any "dip drips" can lead to fun and play. But don't get carried away. This is just the appetizer.

Salad: Prepare a vinaigrette with wine vinegar, olive oil, black pepper, and other seasonings such as dry mustard, or fresh basil. The contents of the salad can vary from chopped vegetables on greens, to bell peppers and feta cheese with greens, to fresh raspberries and melted goat cheese on greens, to peas, mushrooms, and greens, or whatever is light and refreshing. Choose salad ingredients that will quietly appeal to the senses, stimulating the desire for more, rather than heavy foods that are overfilling and kill the appetite just as an aggressive touch or a sexual demand stifles sexual desire.

Entrée: Visual stimulation and pleasing smells are equally important in a meal as well as in a sexual companion. Just as you beautifully prepare and serve each other vegetables, whole-grain pasta or rice, and a fish or light meat well-savored, prepare your bodies for each other too. You may want to shower or bathe together while the meal is cooking. Set the timer so you don't burn your gourmet delight while you enjoy your bodily treat.

When you've finished your main course, take time to totally caress each other's body—the main event of the sexual experience. Take turns. Begin pleasuring each other's back, then the face, hands, feet, and total body. When you have both totally enjoyed the pleasure of caressing your spouse's body, it's time for dessert.

Dessert: A little warm chocolate sauce poured on the chest or breasts is good for dipping and licking. Dip some strawberries in the sauce and feed each other. Papaya or sponge cake dipped into raspberry sauce can be equally delicious and titillating. Dabs of whipped cream with sprinkles of chopped almonds can be strategically placed to invite your spouse to take a taste.

After-Dinner Treats: After-dinner treats are left to the two of you. By now you may want to pursue intercourse or stimulate each other to orgasm, or just laugh and play and hold each other as you go to sleep. Another shower may be necessary so you don't stick to the sheets.

Teaching Touch

Keeping your sex life alive requires teaching time. The main purpose of these events is learning how best to give and get the greatest pleasure and joy. If the experience happens to end up in intercourse, consider it a bonus! In sexual therapy we call these kinds of experiences *nondemand teaching* because they do not demand or expect arousal, orgasm, or intercourse. The only requirement is your willingness to participate and learn.

Begin by bathing or showering together to help you mesh your worlds. Without the goal of stimulation or arousal enjoy one another as you soak in the relaxation. Gently dry each other and proceed to get comfortably in position.

With the man sitting up and leaning comfortably against some pillows, the woman sits between his legs, facing away from him with her back against his chest. You may have to make slight adjustments to one side or the other or slide up or down a bit to accommodate your body-size differences. Husband, begin caressing your wife's face and slowly work your way down her body. The unique ingredient is that the woman guides the man's hands by placing her hands over his. She guides him over her face and neck showing him exactly how she likes to be pleasured. Wife, as you guide his hands over your breasts take some time to communicate the touch you like for pleasure and then for arousal. Be very clear about what kind of touch you like around the areola (the darker area around the nipples) and then the nipples themselves. If you like more (or less) vigorous stimulation as you get aroused, this is a good time to teach your husband what kind of touch you like and when.

If you find the sensitivity of your breasts fluctuating with your hormonal cycles, demonstrate the touch you enjoy at various times of your cycle. Be clear! Practice. Together decide how you will communicate these differences to him.

As you guide him down your abdomen experiment with varying degrees of firmness. Some women become highly aroused as their lower abdomen (between the navel and the public hair line) is firmly caressed. Don't demand that response of yourself but certainly enjoy it if it happens.

It is vital to take some time to teach the caressing of the clitoral area. Many women complain that men are far too vigorous, direct, and fast with their clitoral stimulation and that men don't seem to know when to take a break. Guiding his hand, carefully show him exactly where you like to be touched. Men need to be aware that most women don't like direct stimulation of the head (glans) of the clitoris but rather prefer stimulation around the hood and the shaft of the clitoris. Teach and practice! Enjoy any arousal that occurs.

Using a lubricant, guide his finger gently

around the opening of the vagina to teach him what you like the most. Then guide him by talking and using your hand to guide his as he inserts a finger or two into your vagina. Tighten your Kegel (PC) muscle around his finger. Demonstrate exactly what you like for him to do inside your vagina. If you get highly aroused from G-spot (see Week 49) stimulation, go for it!

In all of this teach him, guide him, talk to him, let him practice, gently adjusting or correcting him, encouraging him, and reinforcing him. Remember: As men get aroused their memory fails so you'll have to teach him some of these points over and over again. Make it fun!

Now it's time to reverse roles. The man teaches the woman what he enjoys, using the same principles and procedures just described. If the man's shoulders are too wide for the woman to reach around, then scoot down and rest your head in her lap while she pleasures your upper body. As much as you can, guide her hands with your hands or at least talk her through the experience. Then shift to your back. Your wife will sit between your legs. In this way she will have easy access to your genitals.

Be very clear in talking and showing her just exactly how you like your penis to be stroked. Discuss how your desire for penile touching changes throughout a sexual experience. Guide her hands! What kind of touch do you like on the underside of the penis (the frenulum)? Is scrotal touch pleasurable or arousing? How much? When?

At the end of this event both of you should clearly know what and when the other one enjoys and where.

If this leads to an orgasm for either of you, great! If not, count it as a delightful way to learn information you will incorporate into your next sexual event. Stop and talk, or proceed to intercourse if that's what you both want.

Surprises

It's time for a few surprises! Independently, either of you take the lead on this one. Plan some events or at least one event that is going to have some surprise to it. Always keep in mind what you already know about your spouse in terms of what he or she responds to or doesn't like. A little embarrassment may enhance the experience, but be careful: Too much will kill it! Never choose something you've been pushing for that offends your spouse.

Tricks: The surprise element makes these fun. It could be anything simple, like having him discover your naked body under the covers (when you usually wear a long flannel nightgown), or something more complicated, like showing up in a gorilla outfit, beating your chest then carrying her off to the guest bedroom.

The tricks could be a tease where there is lots of play but no "pay." Here, either of you could keep provoking the other one's arousal with looks, touching, flirting, titillating, provoking, undressing, playing, whispering, hiding, or whatever you both enjoy. Keep teasing without ever giving in until the very end of the day.

Some people love practical jokes. Occasionally we run into couples who both love being the joker or being on the receiving end. If only one of you enjoys these pranks, forget them! Practical jokes work best when they grow out of some memory, experience, or prior joke. You may short-sheet the bed, have a water fight with hoses or buckets, get him or her with a lemon-meringue pie, or make a suggestive phone call to him or her. The possibilities are endless! But remember: No one should be hurt, offended, slighted, turned off, or humiliated.

Treats: Men, you probably know what she will experience as a treat. Men and women often have very different ideas about what they think is a treat. So whichever one of you is planning and preparing the treat should not necessarily do what *you* would like. Instead, be listening for what would bring the greatest joy to your mate. A man may love to have his wife dance seductively, taking off her clothes for him, but the woman may get nothing if he does the same. Yet, she might really enjoy dancing in the nude with him. The belly rolls that she learned at the belly dancing class will "wind his clock," but his belly rolls may only elicit dieting advice from her. She'd rather do something close.

If she meets him at the front door wearing only a cowboy hat and black boots, he'll love it. But she is much more likely to respond to a bed of flower petals spread all over the carpet in front of the fireplace. A treat for him can certainly include soft, gentle, romantic activity, but he'd usually like to include something that's got some overt, go-for-it sexual intensity to it. While her choice of a treat may include some intense action it will please her most if it starts off with sharing, caressing, and appreciating. Keep in mind that you as a couple may have preferences that are opposite of each other. You may also have different desires than the generalized ones we've described here for men and women. So get to know each other intimately and be responsive to each other's individual fantasies.

Always remember, surprises only brings you together if it brings both of you joy, laughter, and connection.

Something New

New leaders will be elected into office this week, marking the beginning of a new political era. Why not use this time of the year as a reminder to re-vamp or add something new to your sexual experience? Just as political change happens as the result of a candidate's effectively communicating with his or her voters, sexual change will result most logically in response to effective communication between a husband and wife.

To begin the initiation of something new, each of you, individually and separately, answer the following questions on a piece of paper. Divide the paper in half with a vertical line down the middle. On the left side of the paper answer each question in terms of how that particular aspect of the sexual experience is for you now. On the right half of the paper answer how you would like it to be.

1. How do you notice that you are sexually interested?
2. What tends to trigger your desire for sex?
3. How do you let your spouse know you are interested in sex?
4. Who usually initiates your sexual encounter? How? When?
5. How do you handle that initiation if the other

person is not interested in sex? If he or she is interested? Willing?

6. If you proceed with sexual activity, what usually happens next?
7. Do you talk during sex?
8. What sexual activity do you enjoy most?
9. What tends to stimulate or arouse you? Is that comfortable for you?
10. What tends to stimulate or arouse your spouse? Do you enjoy that?
11. When in the process do you reach orgasm? Are you happy with that? What happens if you do not?
12. When in the process does entry occur? Who decides? How do you let each other know when you are ready?
13. What inhibitions keep the two of you from freely enjoying your being together sexually?
14. What happens after intercourse? What do you feel?
15. What one change could you make that would enhance your lovemaking experience?

After each of you has answered these questions, schedule a private, uninterrupted block of time to share your responses with each other. Take turns sharing your answers while the other person listens and reflects back to you what he or she believes you feel about each of the dimensions of your sexual experience. If you have not communicated clearly and have not been understood accurately, clarify or expand. Continue reflecting back and clarifying until you feel heard and understood. And remember that hearing each other does not mean agreeing with each other.

Your answers to these questions could trigger lengthy discussion. Do not hurry the process. Take time to talk through in detail how each of you experiences your sexual process.

After you have shared your responses, select from the right side of each of your papers the parts of your sexual experience you would like to change. On a separate paper, together list those desired changes. Then number them in order of priority. Take the number one issue and make a plan for how you might enhance that particular dimension of your sex life. For example, if you want to change how you express your desire or who initiates or when and how entry occurs, each of you write out your ideas of how that might be put into action. Be very specific. Saying, "I want you to initiate more," may not help. Instead, talk about how often you have sex, how often each of you initiates, and how the other spouse might increase his or her percentage of initiating the sexual experience.

Take one new step at a time. Try your new plan for a designated time period. Schedule a follow-up time to talk about how you are doing. Revise your plan or proceed to the next desired change. Continue this process until both of you are content with the amount of change possible.

Silent Sex

Sexual therapy teaches couples to let go, move vigorously, and make noises. However, sometimes that is not appropriate. When the children, parents, or friends might hear, you need to have silent sex.

Sneaking off to have sex can add fun adrenal-hype to married sex. So this week try the total sexual experience as if Aunt Martha or little Junior were present or listening but would not know what you were doing.

Initiation: One of you may initiate spontaneously when you have the urge, or the two of you can preschedule your time together. Choose whichever works best for your relationship. The only criterion is that the initiation must not be obvious to anyone but the two of you. Keep it a secret!

Pleasuring: Turn off the lights. Pull the shades. Crawl under the covers. There, in the darkness, start hugging and caressing each other very softly and slowly. Take plenty of time to kiss, intensely and passionately. But keep it quiet. No smacking! You can't be obvious to an outsider.

Entry: After you have taken at least twenty or thirty minutes to silently, softly, and intensely pleasure and kiss each other, one of you may suggest entry. If the other is not ready, take more time to caress. Once both of you are ready for entry, pursue entry with both of you on your sides, either facing each other (the lateral position) or with the husband's chest to the wife's back (spoon position). Again, what you are trying to do is have entry so no one would be able to tell what you are doing. Stay under the covers and move without the position of the covers changing.

Thrusting: All movement must be kept slow and controlled so that the bed springs and headboard do not move or creak. Thrusting can be deep and intense, but well managed, so there is no banging sound or obvious sexual noise.

Orgasm: As arousal builds and the urge to respond with sexual moans and groans is felt, enjoy the sensation inside yourself and communicate that feeling to your spouse through the intensity of your touch. As the reflex response of orgasm takes over, respond with a silent scream. Hold tight. Let yourself feel the contractions and the release of the tension. Enjoy every sensation, but keep it between the two of you.

Affirmation: Stay together as long as you can after orgasm and ejaculation. Just hold and enjoy each other. Unobviously, use tissue or a towel to clean up the lubricant and the ejaculate. Whisper sweet messages of love. When you both are ready, fall asleep in each other's arms.

The Big Game

Across the country, the weekend before Thanksgiving is the weekend for cross-town or cross-state football rivals to play the big game of the season.

After the games that interest one or both of you are over, play your own game.

If you are creative, you can make up a fun sexual game. One idea would be for each of you to write out a sexual fantasy. For example, you may have fantasized about being made love to while you were unable to move. So you were totally passive and your spouse was totally active. Or you may have imagined just the opposite—that your spouse let you do anything to him or her and did not move or actively participate. You may have fantasized about having sex outside on the grass or in the backseat of your car or van while parked on a busy street. You may have fantasized about dancing with your spouse in the nude. Whatever your fantasy, write it out, then read each other's fantasy and act it out to the degree that you do not violate either of you, expose yourselves to others, or hurt anyone in any way.

Another game you might create could revolve around throwing dice and thereby winning certain privileges with each other's body. For example, list a number of sexual activities you would enjoy. These could range all the way from a foot caress to kissing, oral stimulation, intercourse, and a magnitude of other options. Assign each activity a number up through twelve. When you roll that number, you get to do or receive the specific sexual treat. You choose whether you wish to be the giver or receiver.

If you find it difficult to create your own game, someone has created one for you. You can order "An Enchanted Evening" from Games Partnership, Ltd., 2040 Laguna Street, San Francisco, California 94115. It is a romantic board game that leads you into some fun and exciting openness and vulnerability with each other regarding your sexual lives. Its context allows you to be as real as you want. It is very safe, yet it can positively impact your sexual life for weeks afterward.

This is your Big Game!

Moments Together

Since it's Thanksgiving week in the United States, you may have difficulty claiming any major block of time for the two of you to explore your forty-seventh sexual prescription of the year. By the end of the week you will probably be fatigued from preparing for guests or a family dinner, visiting with relatives, having children home from school, traveling to visit family, or just from overeating.

This week divide your sexual experience into pieces. Take fifteen minutes each evening to enjoy one piece. Define the boundaries of each evening carefully and don't go beyond that particular activity.

Sunday evening make your plan. Vary it to fit your desires and types of sexual enjoyment, but limit each segment to only one part of your usual sexual experience. Or maybe you want to add a night of engaging in a sexual activity you tend to bypass but would like to have as a more common part of your typical sexual encounter. Include that too. Here's our suggestion for the week's plan:

Monday evening is time to kiss. Reread what you did for Week 31. Practice what you learned in that teaching time. If you found it is more enjoyable or works best if one of you leads the kissing more than the other, have that person lead. If you prefer to take turns leading, that's fine too. Or you may not feel a need for one person to lead. Your kissing may flow back and forth so easily that there is no identifiable leader. Be sure you begin this fifteen-minute kissing time with teeth brushed and flossed and no breath problems. You'll be amazed what fifteen minutes of kissing can do to spark your week.

Tuesday seems like a good night to have fifteen minutes of body rubbing. Set your electronic timer, watch, or alarm for fifteen minutes. When you're getting ready for bed, warm one room of the house. It might be easiest in the bathroom if you have a wall heater or a ceiling heat lamp. Spend your fifteen minutes in the nude, just rubbing your bodies together and hugging each other. If there is arousal, enjoy it, but don't pursue it.

For Wednesday, how about getting your mouths involved again. But this time instead of kissing mouth to mouth, kiss each other's breasts, chest, neck, and upper body.

Thursday will likely be your most tiring day. What often feels great when both spouses are tired and have no sexual energy left is to get into the spoon position with one snuggled behind the other, your chest against the other's back. In this position you can stroke the front of the spouse who has his or her back to your chest. The other one can even guide your hands in that position. You may do the "spooning" in just one direction or you can switch and spoon in the opposite direction for a while. In other words, you can now have your back snuggled against your spouse's chest and he or she can stroke the front of your body with or without your guidance.

By Friday one or both of you may be desiring direct genital stimulation. Depending on your need for warm-up, you may want to have some other closeness first and then spend fifteen minutes patting, affirming, caressing, and stimulating each other's genitals. If that leads to orgasm and ejaculation, enjoy the release. If it does not, enjoy the good sensations.

Saturday finishes your week, so if you are both desirous of intercourse and have the energy to prepare your bodies and spirits for that, go ahead and enjoy! You probably will need more than fifteen minutes. But do keep this one to a "quickie."

Happy Thanksgiving! And remember: When you don't have time to do it all, do what you have time for!

Any Time of Day

Some of you are morning types; others get going about eleven o'clock at night. This makes absolutely no difference unless you happen to be married to someone who is your opposite. Then you've got a challenge! Morning people can be so irritating to evening people. They wake up alert, alive, energized, and ready to go. What's even more irritating, they may be at their sexual finest during the morning wake-up hour! You, on the other hand, may be at your wildest when the clock strikes midnight. If this is your situation, you need to plan a compromise—a nooner!

What we're suggesting here will be a fun twist, even for those couples who operate on the same body clocks, because it is a shift away from the usual. There are two ways to approach this: You can plan it together or one of you can surprise the other.

The surprise means that you show up wherever he or she is at noon under some kind of pretense. If the husband is at home throughout the day (for whatever reason) the wife can take an extra-long lunch hour and show up at the front door, flat-out offering him a "nooner." Or she can be coy and ring the doorbell with a delivery-service hat on. The package she delivers contains a sexy little outfit that will clearly communicate what she has in mind. She could also give him some early warnings by some mysterious phone calls before she arrives home.

Or let's say the wife has been through some stressful times on her job. This is best carried through as a late after-nooner. However, the husband can plan to meet his wife right after work at the office, then show up with a picnic basket full of appetizers. (Make sure you've arranged for someone to take care of your children's dinner. You may be home a little late.)

Lock the office door and enjoy your goodies —and a quickie, or take as long as you have for some pleasuring that may just lead to an orgasm for her or to a slightly risky and exhilarating time of intercourse for the two of you. In all these efforts, bear in mind what you already know about your partner. If either of you is nervous that people might hear, take that into account in what and where you plan your nooner.

It can add a fun dimension to a nooner if you plan it together. This is essential if one of you doesn't like surprises. Also, it may be that your lives are such that the only way you could pull off something like this would be if you plan it together. The jointly planned event could be something as simple as ten minutes at home while you're on your lunch hour or a slow two-hour lunch in a quaint romantic setting that culminates with a half-hour rendezvous on his office floor afterward.

If you plan together you can also design risk or excitement into the event, knowing that the other one will not only go along with the experience but also enjoy it. Again, your nooner could range from simple to elaborate. If you only have a few minutes, you could agree to meet in your van or the family's RV (with curtains closed, of course) in the parking garage at her office or parked on the parking lot at the local mall. You could drive into the middle of a field where you can hear and see everyone coming and make love on a blanket on the grass, in a cornfield, or in the back of your open pickup truck. If you have a little extra time find a secluded place in the woods.

Remember these unusual events only work when both of you can get with the plan rather than one of you talking the other into something that is uncomfortable for him or her. If it brings new excitement, plan it into your life on a regular basis, maybe quarterly.

Also remember that there is nothing sacred about noon. Any time will work. If you can't wait for noon you can always have "funch." That's a nooner, only "sooner" fun—at brunch!

The G-Spot

The G-spot has been the topic of talk shows, the source of much confusion for sexual therapists and physicians, and the elusive hope for nonorgasmic women.

Why all the focus on this particular area in the woman's vagina? A brief history may be helpful. The involuntary sexual responses in our bodies are often a source of frustration for both men and women. We often have the sense that our sexual response is something that happens to us or that we cannot make happen.

For men, this lack of control over sexual response is most associated with erections, the passive response of getting aroused, whereas women tend to be more confused by the active response of sexual release, the orgasm. Why that difference? We are not sure. It may be that women tend to be more passive sexually, so they can more readily soak in the good feelings and allow vaginal lubrication. When they are passive, it may be difficult for them to actively go after an orgasm. Thus, they get stuck right at the point where the involuntary nervous system shifts from passive dominance to active dominance; they often feel like they are about to "go over the hill"—but can't.

Because of the elusive nature of a woman's

orgasm, the professional world has for years attempted to isolate the source of this response. In various studies, women have reported a distinct difference between orgasm from clitoral stimulation and from vaginal stimulation. Some women have even reported orgasmic vaginal response from nipple stimulation or kissing. The clitoris seemed to be left out completely. Then Alice Ladas, Beverly Whipple, and John Perry, the authors of *The G-Spot* compiled more data based on thousands of interviews, letters, and questionnaires, as well as examinations of more than four hundred women. They did not base their findings on observation and measurement of bodily responses.

So what is the G-spot? G is for Grafenberg. Ernst Grafenberg, a German obstetrician and gynecologist, described a bean-shaped erogenous zone in the front wall of the vagina directly behind the pubic bone, that when stimulated by deep pressure, produces vaginal orgasm, distinctly different from clitoral orgasm. He reported discovering this spot in women when he was researching birth control methods in the early 1940s. Ladas, Whipple, and Perry first read about this sensitive area in an article that had been written by Dr. Grafenberg in the *International Journal of Sexology* in 1950.

How can you find this wonderfully responsive area? First, it is essential to understand that no one has proven that every woman even has such an area. Second, this area is difficult for women to find on their own, so this will have to be a joint effort. Third, we have found that many women are not aware of any uniquely pleasurable sensation in that area the first time the search is attempted. These are warnings not to expect miracles and not to be down on yourself if every area in your vagina feels the same to you. Rather, have a good time discovering and playing.

Begin by showering or bathing together. Enjoy washing each other's body. Scrub your fingernails with a brush. You may lotion or oil each other's body. Empty your bladder, since pressing on the G-spot can produce the urge to urinate. Then prop yourself up against the head of the bed in a semi-reclining position. Bend your knees and pull your legs toward your body, so that you are in a squatting position. (The wife can also experiment with this while sitting on the toilet after urinating.)

Making certain your husband has smooth, closely trimmed nails, invite him to gently insert his finger into your vagina to the second knuckle. Have him press on the wall of your vagina, going around the entire "barrel" with varying degrees of pressure. Talk to him about the sensations you experience. With his finger in place, tighten your PC muscle (the muscle that controls the stopping and starting of urination and the tightening and relaxing of the vagina). Have him feel the muscle band tighten around his finger. When he can feel the upper ridge of the PC muscle, have him insert his finger just beyond that edge, and explore the upper front wall of your vagina in the areas just beyond the PC muscle. At the same time he applies firm pressure, strokes, massages, and taps that area, you press your hand downward on the outside of your abdomen, just above the pubic bone. To the finger, the G-spot may feel like a small bean or just like a bumpy area in the vagina. As your husband continues to stroke the area with a firm touch, the area may swell and feel slightly to moderately pleasurable. Enjoy the good feelings and continue the search in future sexual times with either the penis, your finger, or his finger.

Have No Fear

The penis is a wonderful part of human anatomy. But it can also be a scary part, a weapon that can cause much anxiety. It can be enjoyed as a source of love, pleasure, and ecstasy, or avoided as a source of pain and violation. The penis can, at times, seem to have a mind of its own. For example, it may respond (with arousal or ejaculation) when you don't want it to respond, then it may refuse to respond when it's supposed to! To both the man and the woman it can feel like it is separate from the rest of the body. It's out there and it's willful, seeming to do its own thing.

This is the week to talk about, learn about, and experiment with the penis from both the man's and the woman's perspective. If this scares you or makes you uncomfortable, talk about why that happens. Your fear has grown out of messages you've heard or out of past experience because there is nothing to fear about the penis by itself. You will only have developed fears if it was used destructively against you or if it has been surrounded with a dangerous, mysterious aura. In other words, you learned that response from someone else or from your own experience.

Since it's the man's penis, let's have him start the discussion. Husband, talk about your penis. What is your first memory of it? What did you call it as a kid? When do you first remember it as a source of good feelings? Your penis may also have been the source of pain if you had some physical ailment or injury connected with it.

When you reached junior high and started showering in the locker room, was your penis a big issue? How about when you started masturbating? It may have brought both a level of pleasure and a heart full of guilt. What did you do with the guilt?

As a man, have you ever been worried about penis size? In your view was it too short, too long, too thick, or too thin? Or was it too crooked? Talk about it! Be aware that many men unnecessarily worry about penis size. The reality is that the average length is about six inches, give or take an inch or two. Also, note that flaccid, or non-erect, penis size has little to do with the dimension of an erect penis; that is, the smaller flaccid penis tends to increase proportionally more during erection than does the larger flaccid penis. Thus, when erect, most penises are similar in size. You should also know that the longer penis does not bring greater pleasure to a woman since her main pleasure area is just one and one-half to two inches inside the vagina. Also, since the vagina can accommodate various thicknesses, circumference should not be a concern either. Most often the concern about penis size (especially when erect) grows out of hearing male bragging or jokes, 99 percent of which are myths!

When you have shared your attitudes,

memories, and size concerns, talk about any performance anxieties you experience. These would most likely be fear of not getting an erection, fear of losing an erection, or fear of ejaculating too soon (premature ejaculation) or not ejaculating soon enough (retarded ejaculation). Talking about these concerns can be the first step in bringing resolution.

Now let's look at the penis from the woman's perspective. For various reasons, some women have developed a fear of the penis. This may have grown out of violating experiences you suffered or out of a fear of the unknown. Women have some sexual body parts men don't have (breasts, clitoris, etc.), but they don't happen to have anything that sticks out, grows longer, gets harder. Women may also have heard mythical stories that make them fear the penis. Women sometimes associate the man's penis with male aggression. All of this contributes to the caution or fear some women exhibit toward the penis.

In previous weeks we have suggested ways to make the "little guy" your friend. This would be a good time to talk to him using the name you gave him a few weeks ago, stroke him, give him a kiss —make him yours! Remember, the penis is for your pleasure. If you can't enjoy the penis, talk about it! What is your history around the penis? When did you first see one? What was your reaction? If the penis was a source of fear or violation, talk about it. You may need professional help to get past abuse if that was part of your life. What adolescent penis experiences did you have? How did it impact today's reactions? What kind of stories did you hear about the penis? Is size (too big or too small) an issue for you? Is it hard for you to touch a flaccid or erect penis? Do you know why? If you are "in love" with "Charlie," how did you get that way?

The penis is one of our Creator's sexual gifts to women, so think of it as yours to enjoy, to play with, and to invite into you for your special pleasure. The penis is also the primary source of sexual pleasure for the man. So husband, bask in your wife's playfulness and take in all the moist love and warmth as she invites you in.

Cozy Christmas Time

Christmas is the time of the year when we sip hot wassail, sit by a crackling fireplace, and connect with our loved ones. We think of celebrating through joyful music, the giving of gifts, and the sharing of festive meals. We picture Christmas greens, sparkling lights, candles, and beautiful decorations. All of this reminds us of the gift of relationships that are possible because of the gift of Jesus.

With that background, come to your time together this week focusing on the gift of yourselves to each other. Plan into your experience the warmth of sipping a hot drink together in front of the fireplace at the end of Christmas Day after everyone else has left or gone to bed. Don't worry about cleaning up. Take time to connect. Celebrate your relationship by playing your favorite music. Look at your home, so beautifully decorated. Take in the beauty of this atmosphere that fills your home once a year. Then give yourselves the gift of each other.

Snuggle up and talk to each other about your love. Tell your spouse how you show your love for him or her. When you have described your ways of *expressing* love, think about how you *sense* your spouse's love for you. Each of you complete this statement: "I know you love me when you _____." Talk about other ways you might show love or know that you are loved. Many times couples miss each other's messages of love because they fail to clarify their differences in sending those messages. They erroneously assume that their expressions of love are obvious to the spouse. So the bow is bent and the love arrow is released, but the arrow misses the target.

When you are both ready to go to bed, snuggle into each other's arms. Softly kiss, hug, and stroke each other. Enjoy the closeness and warmth without proceeding to orgasm or intercourse. Fall asleep together. Merry Christmas! And to all a good night.

Winter Retreat

Can you believe this is the last week of your year of experimenting with fun, fantastic sex? Take some time this week to individually and separately reflect on the past year.

Each of you go through the book and list the weeks' experiences into various categories. For example, you may make lists for those you enjoyed most, those you need to repeat, those you wish to repeat, and those that you'd like to incorporate into your ongoing sex life. Then share your lists with each other and together compile a list that is agreeable to both of you. Use this list to create a "master plan" for your sexual future.

But the fun isn't over yet! We've got one more suggestion for fun, fantastic sex for you—if you're feeling hearty.

Plan a brief winter retreat for you and your spouse—outside! Sure, we know it may be cold where you live. But that's the fun of it. What could be cozier than being *truly* warmed by each other's body? Just be sure to leave the door unlocked so you can get back inside when the fun is over. If you live in a warmer climate, you may have to improvise by *pretending* you're in a cold, wintry place (and cranking up the air conditioning for a couple of hours).

Here's what you do: Buy, borrow, or rent a double sleeping bag. (After the past year of fun, fantastic sex, maybe you already own one!) During the afternoon, plan where you will have your night-time retreat: in a tent in the backyard, in the back of a pickup or van, or even on the back porch or the balcony of your apartment. Have everything ready. If you don't, you'll back out. It may be fun to have sex outside when it's cold and dark, but it's *not* fun to pitch a tent!

When the kids are sound asleep and the night is good and dark, slip out of your clothes and into a robe or something else you can get in and out of quickly and easily. Then head for the sleeping bag. It may be a little tricky getting out of your robe and into the bag without getting frostbitten or spotted by your neighbors. But that's part of the fun. Then, when you're both in the bag together . . .

Well, by now we believe you know what to do!

About the Authors

Dr. Clifford and Joyce Penner are internationally recognized sexual therapists, educators, and authors. They work as a team in full time practice in sex therapy and counseling. They also lead sexual enhancement weekends for couples and lecture on human sexuality at colleges and universities.

Joyce, a native of Minnesota, is a registered nurse and clinical nurse specialist. She holds a B.S. in nursing from the University of Washington and a master's degree in psychosomatic nursing and nursing education from UCLA.

A native of Canada, Clifford is a clinical psychologist. He earned a B.A. from Bethel College, a M.A. in theology from Fuller Theological Seminary, and a Ph.D. from Fuller's Graduate School of Psychology.

The Penners have authored five books on sexuality and recently produced a video series on enhancing sexual communication, called "The Magic and Mystery of Sex." To contact them, write:

Clifford and Joyce Penner
2 North Lake Avenue, Suite 610
Pasadena, CA 91101